Carving Faces And Figures In Wood

E.J. Tangerman

Sterling Publishing Co., Inc.   New York

Oak Tree Press Co., Ltd London & Sydney

About the Author

E. J. Tangerman has been carving for over 50 years and has written a number of seminal reference books, including "Whittling and Woodcarving," regarded as the basic text in the field. He has also written numerous articles for such magazines as *Popular Mechanics* and *Popular Science Monthly*. Mr. Tangerman is currently vice-president of the National Wood Carvers Association.

Photographs of Yugoslav art courtesy of Smithsonian Institution, Traveling Exhibition Service, Washington, D.C. 20560.

Contents

You Can Carve the Human Figure 5

Chapter I: How to Choose and Use Tools 6

Chapter II: How to Choose the Wood 15

Chapter III: The Question of Size 18

Chapter IV: How to Carve a Face—and Head 22

Chapter V: Carve a Caricature 38

Chapter VI: Who Took the "A" Train? 47

Chapter VII: As We Carve Ourselves (Native Figures) 53

Chapter VIII: The South American Approach 61

Chapter IX: Naive Art in Yugoslavia 69

Chapter X: Flowing Figures from Bali 73

Chapter XI: Base or No Base—Which? 79

Chapter XII: How About Surface Textures? 81

Chapter XIII: Composites and Assemblies 88

Chapter XIV: High Relief Permits Realistic Scenes 93

Chapter XV: Lower Relief and Modelling 101

Chapter XVI: How to Carve Nudes 113

Chapter XVII: An Action Sports Figure 119

Chapter XVIII: The Self-Made Man 123

Index 128

Fig. 1. "Widows" was carved by Dorde Kreća, a Yugoslav carver. It shows two women seated back to back, and was carved from a single stump. It is 33¾ in (84 cm) tall. See Chapter IX.

You Can Carve the Human Figure

THE HUMAN FIGURE is probably what we know most intimately and think we know best. Other things around us—animals, flowers, man-made and other inanimate objects—impinge upon us and we know them after a fashion. We give them human attributes and describe human attributes with them interchangeably. Other elements—heat, cold, rain, distance, mountains, water, fire, etc.—affect our well-being, so we interpret or represent them in various ways, but basically we relate everything else to ourselves. This is particularly true of primitive artists.

It follows that the most interesting subject for a whittler or a woodcarver is the human figure. Many of the carvings pictured in this book are primitive, but they are basic as well. They show much more graphically than words the many approaches and attempted solutions to the problem we know best, yet never solve—ourselves. This book tries to provide answers, both by supplying basic proportions and techniques, as well as by showing how woodcarvers all over the world have solved the problem, or have tried to solve it.

We who have always had trouble carving the human form can take heart from the knowledge that we are not alone. A few of us, gifted with a second sight, are able to carve the human form or face with little difficulty. For the rest, it is a slow and painful process. But that is no reason to abandon the effort; the way to make a good human body, or a good human face, is to make one after another until they approach what our inner eye sees.

The content of this book is graded from relatively simple to complex. Both in-the-round and panel carving are included, with some step-by-step photographs and patterns for many of the figures discussed. Instructions and hints are as thorough as I could make them. Sizes range from miniature to heroic and figures vary widely in pose, dress, age and even emotion. I hope they will encourage you to try, and to keep on trying. You will find the effort as rewarding as I have.

E. J. Tangerman

5

CHAPTER I

How to Choose and Use Tools

IF YOU ARE JUST STARTING TO CARVE, you can't beat a knife and a piece of pine or basswood. The great convenience of the pocketknife or clasp knife is that you can take it with you and set up shop whenever you're so inclined. A knife with a fixed handle is safer for cutting (the blade won't snap shut on your finger) but a nuisance to carry; its edge must be protected against all things hard or soft. Its handle is bigger and more comfortable, but you need a sheath to carry it. The knife should be of good quality and have a carbon-steel blade, rather than stainless. It will rust if you don't keep it lightly oiled, but it will also hold an edge longer, which is important unless you long to carry a hone and a lap with you as well. As to blade shape and size, you'll find that you seldom need a blade longer than 1½ in (4 cm); a longer blade will bend and your hand is too far back to control it as well. A knife with one long blade with a sharp point (*saber* or *B-clip*) and a smaller one with a stubbier tip (*pen*) is the basic answer. It can have three blades, but shouldn't have more than that or the knife becomes too clumsy. I usually carry two knives—one with pen, spear, and B-clip, the other with pen and B-clip (Fig. 2). The three-bladed knife is larger and has wider blades, so will take heavier cuts; the small blade handles the delicate and hard-to-get-at spots and shallow concavities. The small blade is more likely to break and harder to control, as well as slower, but the big blades get in their own way on occasion.

Wood has grain and tends to splinter and split along it. It is much easier to cut with the grain than across it, of course (those long curling chips are cut with the grain), but a tree is a living thing and its grain may not be straight, or it may veer around damage or a knot. The first thing you must learn is to keep the grain in mind at all times. If you cut with it, it's easy; if you cut squarely across it, it's harder work but no problem with splitting; but watch out if you cut *into* the grain, because even the thin wedge of a knife blade may cause splitting and will certainly cause some roughness. The problem varies with the wood: basswood and white pine offer fewer problems

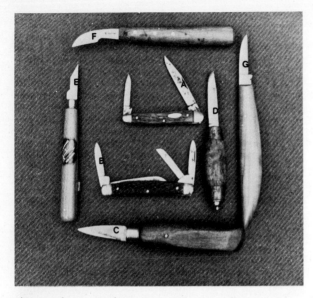

Fig. 2. Typical knives for woodcarving include: A, *a penknife with pen and B-clip blades, and* B, *a slightly larger one with pen, spear, and cut-off pen. Both are German-made. Below them is* C, *an inexpensive fixed-blade knife, and to the right is a Swedish sloyd,* D. *The others are specialized shapes:* E *and* F *are used for chip carving;* G *is a German fixed-blade knife.*

than ash or mahogany, teak less than walnut. You will learn about grain quickly and soon appreciate the necessity for cutting in the opposite direction on the into-grain side of even a slightly diagonal groove.

The standard cartoon of a whittler shows him paring off big chips with bold strokes going away from himself. That is very safe but produces only chips. The most important cut for the knife is exactly like that used by someone peeling a potato: the knife caught in the curve of the four fingers, the thumb on the work, and the cut made by closing the hand. That gives the greatest control because it is finger rather than arm muscle that does the work. (While you're learning this cut, be careful of your thumb.) Other frequent cuts are made with the thumb or the forefinger extended along the heel of the blade to provide added force just behind the cut itself. Or the knife may be gripped like a dagger and drawn or pushed to make a slice—this is an arm-muscle cut, so control is poorer. Another type of cut is that in which the point of the knife is pushed into the wood, then the knife is rocked or rotated, in the first case to make a triangular incision and in the second to make a cone-shaped depression.

Some cuts are better done by using the thumb or forefinger of the other hand to push and guide the blade. This is very helpful with harder woods and ivory because the actual cutting force can be so exactly controlled. The cut, in any case, is very short because the hand itself will be gripping or resting on the work.

Woodcarvers use more tools

BASIC TOOLS of the woodcarver are *chisels* with either flat or curved edges, pushed by hand or driven by *mallet*, depending upon the hardness of the wood and on personal preference. Chisels in general are shorter and lighter than carpenter's chisels of the same width and are available in many more degrees of curvature, of both edge and shank. They are often supplemented by *rasps* for rough work in soft woods and by *riffler files* (small, shaped files) for smoothing details.

The carver's flat chisel is called a *firmer* (*F*, Fig. 3), and differs from a carpenter's chisel in that it is sharpened from both sides, so it is less inclined to dig in. It can be obtained in widths from ¹⁄₁₆ to 2 in (1.6 to 50 mm). Edge is usually perpendicular to the side, but some have the edge at an angle and are called *skews* (*A*, Fig. 4). The skew is commonly used by European carvers much as we use a knife; they hold it by the blade rather than the handle for such work. Curved chisels are called *gouges* (*B*, *E*, Fig. 3), and can range from quite flat curves to a U-shape. The smallest U-shaped gouge, usually ¹⁄₁₆ in (1.6 mm) across the flat side, is called a *veiner* (*D*, Fig. 3), from the work it often does. The next size, ⅛ in (3.2 mm), is called a *fluter* —for the same reason. The very large ones are usually used for rough-shaping (up to 2½ in, or 6 cm, wide) although they can also smooth broad, curved surfaces in finishing. A modified firmer, called the *bullnose* (*G*, Fig. 3; *C*, Fig. 4), is being used increasingly by amateurs for shaping; it is simply a firmer with the corners rounded off, so that the edge is a flat arc.

There are a number of specially shaped chisel edges designed for particular jobs. Most familiar is the *parting*, or *V-tool*, shaped as its name implies (*C*, Fig. 3). It is used for outlining and for cutting accurate V-grooves, although one edge will tend to dig in and tear in diagonal cuts unless it is extremely sharp. Another is the *macaroni*, which cuts a channel that is flat on the bottom and square on the sides. Similar is the *fluteroni*, which cuts a smaller trench with arcuate corners.

Wide tools, and some narrower ones, are tapered down to the tang (which enters the handle). These are called *spades* or *fishtails* (*A*, Fig. 3; *B*, Fig. 4) and get into tight places better. The shank may also be forged into a long (*long-bent*) or a short (*short-bent*) curve near the blade (*A*, *C*, Fig. 5) to get into pockets or to undercut (the continuing problem of the woodcarver is clearance for his tools). There is also a *back-bent* tool shape, which is necessary, for example, to undercut individual grapes of a bunch, if you specialize in grapes. For small work there are shorter chisels with handles that

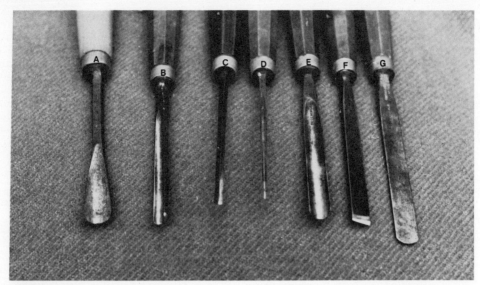

Fig. 3. Typical chisel shapes: A, 1-in (25.4-mm) #9 spade gouge; B, ½-in (12.7-mm) #10 gouge; C, ¼-in (6.3-mm) V-tool; D, veiner; E, ½-in (6.3-mm) #7 gouge; F, ½-in (12.7-mm) firmer; G, ⅝-in (16-mm) bullnose firmer.

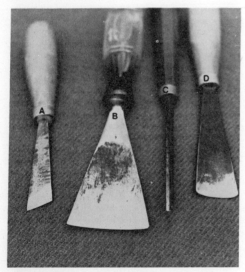

Fig. 4. Shorter tools include: A, 1-in (25.4-mm) skew firmer with homemade spade shank; B, 2½-in (6-cm) #5 spade gouge; C, ½-in (12.7-mm) bullnose #7 gouge; D, 1½-in (3-cm) #5 gouge.

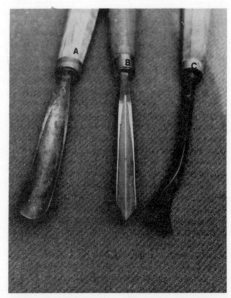

Fig. 5. Special shapes: A, 1-in (25.4-mm) long-bent #9 gouge; B, ¾-in (19-mm) spade V-tool; C, short-bent #5 gouge.

fit the palm of the hand, as does the shoemaker's awl or the engraver's burin. In modern days, most carvers stick to fairly low relief, so tools such as these specials are not necessary. The bent gouges, for example, have a tendency to spring and are hard to sharpen.

Carving tools are either held in one hand and struck with a mallet in the other, or pushed with one hand and guided and restrained with the other, so the work must be held or supported in some way. Oriental carvers put it in their laps and may lock a knee over a three-dimensional piece. Big panels will easily rest on a flat surface, while smaller ones can be set against a backboard, benchplate (Fig. 6), or wooden vee on a bench. It is also possible simply to nail (through waste wood) a panel to a surface, or to hold it in a vise. For 3-D pieces, however, European carvers long ago invented the *carver's screw*, which is screwed into the base of the work through a hole in the bench, then locked with a wingnut. (I have never found one necessary.)

Mallets were once shaped like wooden potato mashers (mine still are), but I've seen wood hammers, soft-faced hammers, and clubs of various sorts used. Nowadays, there are plastic-faced mallets, lead or babbit-metal mallets, rubber-faced mallets—whatever suits a particular carver's preferences. I use a light mallet for more exact control of many cuts. Other carvers do these by hand, but I have found that several weights of mallet will work as well.

What tools to buy is largely a matter of personal preference or availability when you start. As you learn, you will buy the tools you particularly need for what you prefer to do. I started with a kit of nine tools, several of which I have never used—or almost never. Authorities offer various lists, but these are based on their own teaching methods. Charles M. Sayer, who taught panel carving, suggests four initial tools: ½-in (12.7-mm), or ⅜- to ⅝-in (9.6 to 16-mm) No. 39 parting tool; ⅝-in (16 mm) No. 5 straight gouge; 1-in (25-mm) or ⅞-in (22.4-mm) No. 3 straight gouge; and ⅜-in (9.6-mm) No. 7 straight gouge. For relief carving, he adds a ⅜-in (9.6-mm) No. 3 straight gouge. H. M. Sutter, who has taught carving for the past 30 or 40 years, starts his students with five tools, plus an all-purpose carver's knife: ⅜-in (9.6-mm) No. 3 straight gouge; ⅝-in (16-mm) No. 5 straight gouge (these two preferably fishtail); ⅜-in (9.6-mm) No. 9 straight gouge; 1-mm or ¹⁄₃₂-in No. 11 veiner; and a ⅜-in (9.6-mm) No. 1 parting or V-tool. Note that neither suggests fancy shapes or skew chisels to start.

The numbers, by the way, refer to the so-called London system of identification in which a firmer is No. 1, a skew firmer 2, a flat gouge 3, and a

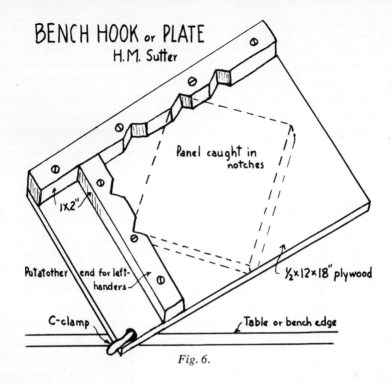

BENCH HOOK or PLATE
H.M. Sutter

Panel caught in notches

1×2"

Put at other end for left-handers

½×12×18" plywood

C-clamp

Table or bench edge

Fig. 6.

U-shaped gouge 11 or 12, with the other arcs in between. Other numbers are used by certain suppliers for special tools or for their own catalog identification, but most also show a cross-section of the various sweeps or radii. Also, carving tools made on the Continent are sized in millimeters: 1, 2, 3, 4, 5, 6, 7, 8, 10, 12, 16, 20, 25, 30, 35 mm wide, etc. (1 mm = 0.039 in). The English system has tools from $\frac{1}{16}$ to $\frac{3}{8}$ in (1.6 to 3.2 mm) in sixteenths, then in larger steps up to the 2½-in (6 cm) maximum.

My best advice is to start with a limited set from a reputable supplier. Find out how they work, what you prefer to make, and what tools work best for you. You don't need a golfbag full of clubs to make a round. You'll need a flat gouge for roughing, shaping and cleaning up; a firmer for carving flat surfaces and angles; a veiner for outlining and emphasizing lines and/or a V-tool for similar purposes; as well as a gouge or two of varied sweeps for making concave curves. As you progress, add gouges and a skew chisel, but vary gouge size considerably; if you have a $\frac{3}{8}$-in (9.6-mm), don't get a ½-in (12.2-mm) of the same sweep. For heavy work, carpenter's chisels and gouges are cheaper.

I find chisels easier to learn to use than the knife. The cutting edge is narrower and less versatile and it is pushed directly instead of being used in an arc by finger or arm power. If you use a mallet, you must obviously learn to watch the chisel edge, not the head of the mallet. You must learn to take it easy and not try to remove all the waste wood on the first pass. You must learn to adjust the angle of the tool as you cut so it doesn't run in and stick or run out and slip. You start cutting at an edge and work toward the middle; if you cut to an edge, the chisel will break out and tear the wood. Learn at once how to cut across grain with a gouge. Learn to be ambidextrous with the chisels. If you are planning a panel with a background, practice *setting in* or *bosting* before you try it on the panel. (First, you outline the background space with a veiner or V-tool, then you drive in firmers and flat gouges along this groove to limit the cut. Then, and only then, attempt to cut out wood with a gouge. These steps must be taken in order or you will gouge into the design, or the outlining firmer will crush surface fibres and mess up the sharp edge of the design.)

Your constant challenge will come from the grain of the wood. In any diagonal cut, for example, one edge of the gouge will cut cleanly, the other will drag and tear the wood slightly because it is cutting into the grain. You'll learn how to cope with this and soon will be adjusting automatically for it. The other major point is to keep your tools razor-sharp, particularly for cutting soft woods—so you'll have to learn how to sharpen. Makers of whetstones provide literature on the basics of this. (*See* Fig. 7 for typical sharpening equipment.)

Some general hints

WHEN YOU ARE USING either knife or chisel, try to avoid wedging out the chip; you may break the tool or split the wood. Obviously, tools are not to be used for cutting newspaper clippings, paring nails, or peeling electrical insulation; all these destroy the cutting edge. The old professionals laid their chisels out with the edges toward themselves, so they could select the right chisel easily. I find this hard to do because it requires reversal of the tool when you pick it up and when you lay it down. Some carvers put distinguishing marks on handles for rapid identification of frequently used tools.

Leave a light film of oil on the tools after use—it will reduce rusting. This is particularly true of pocketknives: sweat can be very corrosive. Keep tools very sharp. Store them out of reach of the curious, old and young, and keep the edges protected if you carry them about.

There are canvas and leather rolls available for carrying tools, or you can make them yourself. For storage, tools can be racked or placed in slots in a drawer. It is a good idea to hone a chisel after you've used it extensively, but do not strop it until you use it again; a stropped edge deteriorates rapidly, as any barber will tell you. Also, in sharpening, don't change the cutting angle without reason. Presumably, your tools were sharpened to the basic

Fig. 7. *Sharpening equipment includes (clockwise from top): a round-edge roughing stone, an impregnated-rubber (flexible) fine-grit, two Arkansas slips, and a leather strop mounted on plywood.*

15° angle when you got them. As you hone, you will probably widen that angle slightly because you tend to create a chisel edge. This is all right, but periodically it will be necessary to hone away metal from the entire cutting face to match the edge wear. Don't grind a tool unless you've chipped or broken the cutting edge or want to change it; grinding can draw temper or burn the cutting edge, among other drawbacks.

Lastly, if you nick yourself, protect the cut, because you may find you'll repeat the nicking. This is particularly true of the ball of the thumb when you make small carvings with paring cuts. It may be advisable to use a finger stall initially; stationery stores sell rubber ones that are used by people who sort papers.

The proper way to carve is to stand at a high bench or stand that is heavy enough so it doesn't shift under the mallet blows. Some sculptors have four-legged stands that are weighted with a rock toward the bottom, with the top adjustable for height, possibly even incorporating a lockable lazy Susan so it can be rotated. Panel carvers, like those who work on cuckoo-clock frames, have sloping tables with 2-in (5-cm) tops and pins to index and hold the work. I work on a trestle table on the terrace, a basement bench, or even on a bridge table. I sit down whenever possible. The main thing is to have a stable surface that will absorb mallet blows, with some sort of adjacent surface on which your tools may be placed. For any given job, you rarely need more than ten or a dozen tools. You can have whatever sort of bench or stand that suits your ego, and as many tools as you like, but a solid surface and good light, plus some air, suit me best.

Personally, I don't need a studio.

CHAPTER II

How to Choose the Wood

"WHAT WOOD SHOULD I USE?" is a common neophyte question, and one often asked by the sculptor undertaking work in wood as well, particularly if the sculpture is to be heroic in size. If you are a neophyte, you'd best start with basswood, soft white pine, or jelutong (now being imported from Indonesia). All are essentially similar in color and reaction to tools, although many whittlers prefer the basswood, if they can get it.

Here is a counter-question: "What sources of wood are available to me?" If it's only the local lumberyard, you have problems, because they probably don't stock basswood and their white pine may not be first grade. Also, thickness is likely to be 2 in (5 cm) at most, so you may have to glue up a laminated block for anything over that. Basswood may grow in your area and be known as *bee tree* (it's similar to European linden). It is soft, colorless, and doesn't split excessively. Ponderosa pine or sugar pine are almost as good. Avoid strongly colored pieces of the former. These woods are easy to work, but they don't hold detail very well and tend to break down if handled. Also, they are lifeless when finished in natural color; they're better painted or tinted. One caution: avoid yellow pine, which is hard, knotty, resinous, and tends to split.

Several other woods are commonly used for simple carvings, including poplar (bruises easily and tends to grip tools), cedar (its color may be a problem), and willow (watch out for splitting). Balsa may be good for models, but is unfit for carving. Old-time whittlers tended to use whatever was available, depending upon what they planned to make. (Some present-day carvers also scrounge.) In general, they tended to harder woods, particularly the fruits and nuts: pear, pecan, cherry, apple, walnut. All of these tend to check in large pieces, but they will take detail and finish more interestingly without color. Black walnut is without doubt the best American carving wood. It has a fine, tough grain, takes detail well, and doesn't have too much tendency to split. However, it is quite dark when finished.

If you can find them, butternut, red alder and myrtle are much softer than walnut and easier to carve. Redwood is quite soft and may alternate layers of hard and soft wood (winter and summer growth are at different rates); this makes trouble. Sweet or red gum is durable, but tends to warp and twist. I have carved ash with good results, although it is stringy. Cypress is good, particularly for large figures exposed to the air; it can be carved green because it has little tendency to shrink or check. Beech, hickory, sycamore and magnolia are all hard to cut and recommended only for shallow carving. Birch and rock or sugar maple are hard to carve and finish, but durable. Soft maple (commonly stocked by suppliers) is not a good carving wood. Eastern white oak is inherently strong and will take detail, but should be carved with tools. Swamp or red oak has a very prominent grain and coarse structure: avoid it. Dogwood is very dense and hard and can stand shock without splitting, but it is difficult to carve. Holly, our whitest wood, is hard and tends to check, but it holds detail well. In the Southwest, there are mesquite, ironwood and osage orange, all very hard, inclined to split and difficult to carve, but finish beautifully.

The imported woods, if you can get them, offer much more variety in color and figure or grain, but they tend to be as hard as walnut, or harder, so are not for the neophyte, the impatient, or the slapdash. Also, they are much easier to carve with chisels and in some cases with power equipment. The exception perhaps is mahogany, which is not one wood, but a whole series, some not even members of the same family. Quality and color vary with source and individual piece. Honduras mahogany is fine-grained and relatively soft; Cuban is dense and varies in hardness; South American likely to be grainy and splintery. Philippine mahogany has a reputation for coarseness, but can vary widely: I have samples ranging from white to dark red and coarse to dense; the heaviest is double the weight of the lightest. Other woods sold as mahogany include luanda. Primavera cuts like mahogany and can be stained to be indistinguishable from it. It is a white wood, hence is called white mahogany.

Teak, which comes from Burma or Thailand, is my favorite carving wood, particularly for panels. It is a warm brown, with little visible grain, and not subject to insect attack, warpage or dry rot. It does not vary or check to any degree and so is excellent for exposed carving. It is about like walnut to carve, but contains an oil that makes the tools slip through it easily, but do not be surprised to find that it dulls tools rapidly. This occurs because the wood grows in swamps and apparently draws up fine silica with the water—as our own holly draws up black dirt to become grey rather than white.

Chinese teak is not brown, but red and harsh-grained, which is why the Chinese enameled it black and most Americans think of teak as a shiny black wood, just as they assume that all black African carvings are ebony. (Many are now softer woods, stained or painted.) Ebony, which grows in Africa, India, Ceylon (now Sri Lanka), Indonesia, and South and Central America, varies in color from black (Gabon, from Africa) to dark brown with lighter striping (Macassar, from Indonesia, or Calamander, from Ceylon). Like lignum vitae and cocobola (lignum vitae in Mexico and Central America is guayacan), ebony is very hard and used primarily by sculptors willing to work hard per chip. Ebony, however, is the only black wood.

English sycamore (harewood) is like our holly and available in wider boards. Lacewood, satinwood, briar, sandal, purpleheart (heat it to make it purple), bubinga, vermilion (very crimson), and others will take fine detail but are very expensive—I use them for elements of mobiles and for pendants. They can be whittled, but you'd best know your stuff. Rosewood, which comes from many southern countries, varies from soft brown through dark red to red-brown and almost purple, with other colors thrown in (Mexico). This is a beautiful wood, but quite hard to carve and tends to give a heavy effect. Save it for pieces in which color and grain will not defeat your carving. Most expensive of woods is pink ivory, from Africa, once the private wood of Zulu kings. It is very hard, like ebony, and pinkish to red.

Finally, start with familiar and easy woods and work up to the others. The exotic woods make wonderful carvings, but take much in sweat, blood and tears. I have indicated, piece by piece, my choice of wood—or that of other carvers—throughout this book. Also, regardless of wood, avoid a blank with knots, flaws or checks if you can. Knots take the edge off tools and may fall out later. Both knots and flaws require some skill at finishing. Checks have a disconcerting way of opening and closing with humidity changes, and filling a check to hide it may cause pressure that will crack the piece later.

CHAPTER III

The Question of Size

How to decide it, and how to get a pattern to fit

USUALLY, THE SIZE of a figure carving is dictated by the size of the wood available, not so much its length, but its width or thickness. Lumber is 1 or 2 in thick (25.4 or 51 mm), which means a ⅞- or 1¾-in (22.4-or 44-mm) planed thickness. Widths are arbitrary 1, 2, 3 or 4 in, again reduced by planing. So, after you've selected the figure you want to carve, measure its maximum dimension and enlarge or reduce your drawing or photograph to fit the maximum dimension to the wood.

Generally, wood size is unimportant. If you are fortunate and can select, size is largely a matter of taste. If you are planning to sell the pieces, the larger it is, the more you can charge for it in general. Secondly, the larger the piece, the easier it is to carve detail and the less trouble you'll have with grain in complex areas, but also the more waste wood you'll have to remove. (Carving time really isn't reduced much by reducing size—as you approach a miniature, carving time will actually increase.) Thirdly, think of where and how the piece is to be displayed or used: big carvings soon fill all available space, and small carvings tend to be lost amid the larger decorations of a room. Fourth, a large carving tends to require less support because it has enough mass to resist even mallet blows; it does, however, require larger tools and a greater ability to get around it, and has a greater tendency to check. If you are whittling, you can't hold a large piece in your hand, and the whittling seems to go much more slowly as a result.

All in all, I would say that a figure 6 or 8 in tall (15.2 or 20.3 cm) is about right for whittling. It can be twice that size for carving with chisels. In this book most carvings are sketched at about half size, to provide some clue as to the taste (or wood availability) of the original maker. If you double the size of the drawings, you'll have the original size of the piece, unless a footnote specifies a different one (usually larger).

To convert the pattern to the desired size, the fastest method is to have the drawing photostatically enlarged. Most copying machines make only

Figs. 8 and 9. This shepherd from Oberammergau (above) is 6 in (15 cm) tall, but has a thin base—which looks good but is difficult to shape well. "Justice," an heroic 10-ft (3-m) figure, was carved of pine over a century ago to top a courthouse tower, and now is in the Shelburne (Vt.) Museum.

same-size copies, but there is probably a local commercial shop that does photostatting, and some of the newer copying machines can enlarge or reduce also. If you can take a photo of the drawing, you can blow it up in an enlarger and either print or copy to desired size, or you can project a transparency to any desired size and trace the image.

If none of these methods fits the situation, I customarily make a point-to-point outline sketch (*see* Fig. 10). I put top or base and side reference lines on the original at right angles to each other, and make all measurements from them. Similar base and side reference lines are put on the wood or another sheet of paper. Then I locate key points of the pattern by measuring from the base and side lines to that point on the original, multiplying the measurements by the enlargement or reduction factor, and locating the matching point on the copy. Obviously, it is easiest to double or triple the size, or to halve it; otherwise, the mathematics become too involved and the risk of error is great. If I'm doubling the size, for example, let's assume the point I am locating is 1½ in (3.8 cm) from the side and 4¼ in (10.8 cm) from the bottom. I measure 2 × 1½ = 3 in (7.6 cm) from the side and 2 × 4¼ = 8½ in (21.6 cm) from the bottom. When a number of such points have been located, lines of the proper shape are drawn to connect them.

POINT-to-POINT METHOD

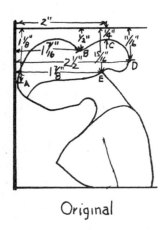

Original

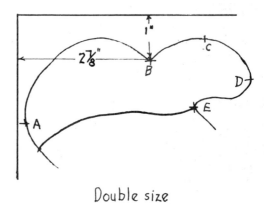

Double size

Fig. 10.

If you feel a bit shaky about the point-to-point method, use the method of squares (Fig. 11). On the original, or on a sheet of plastic, draw a grid of ⅛-in (3 mm) squares, big enough to cover the original, of course. On the wood, or on a sheet of paper, draw a corresponding grid of squares that gives

20

you the desired enlargement (¼ in [6 mm] for double size, ⅜ in [9 mm] for triple size). Now copy the drawing square by square. It sounds slow and difficult, but is really quite fast and accurate, and the transparent template can be saved for reuse on other pieces.

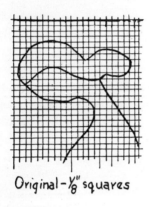

Original - ⅛" squares

Fig. 11.

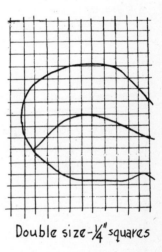

Double size - ¼" squares

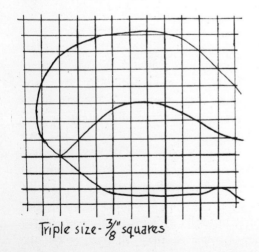

Triple size - ⅜" squares

METHOD of SQUARES

CHAPTER IV

How to Carve a Face – and Head

"HOW DO I CARVE A FACE?" is probably the most common question asked by woodcarvers intent upon improving their work. Unlike some other operations in the art, there is no simple answer here. This question leads to a question in reply: "What kind of a face do you want to carve?"

Caricature and "Western-style" carvings come closest to having a standard formula—most use a series of notches and surfaces to suggest facial contours. The competent caricaturist tends to develop his own style, often based upon his own countenance, and tends to repeat the head in the same position and with the same expression until it becomes a stereotype. Further, a great many such faces are not caricatures as much as three-dimensional cartoons or, more properly, grotesques—they rely for their humor upon a gross distortion of one facial feature, usually the nose. Such a face can be carved rapidly, with little practice, and its deficiencies in detail are compensated for by judicious touching up with paint or ink. To the serious carver, such a face eventually becomes trite. He seeks expression, likeness, normalcy, and comes to realize, as a sculptor friend remarked, "Caricature is a cop-out."

And well it may be. We all use the face as the most important recognition feature among humans. We establish race, mood, background, experience, state of health among strangers and identity among friends. We worry about the "face we present to the world." We know a great deal about the face, which we normally look at first and longest when we meet someone, so we set a higher standard for its proper reproduction. A carved figure can be misproportioned, awkwardly posed, or otherwise distorted and we are not particularly conscious of it, but we are immediately conscious of any error in a face, however small. What's more, we have memorized an endless number of stereotypes for races, for nationalities, for ages, and particularly for specific individuals. We have a catalog of images for historical figures based largely upon the face—for Jesus, Washington, Churchill, Lincoln, Jefferson, Napoleon, Franklin, and an endless number of other people—all from some particular portrait or traditional description.

The individual may, in point of fact, have differed markedly from the accepted facial image, but both his face (and his age!) are now fixed by convention. You can vary his body structure and even his clothing with some impunity and few are likely to notice, but change the face even slightly and even your friends will dismiss the carving as faulty.

There is, for most of us, a long and painful process before the achievement of good faces. No formula will help us beyond the initial stages. One can memorize facial proportions and a series of steps in carving and still not produce memorable faces for a very long time. This may be, in fact, one area in which there is no alternative for apprenticeship; that is, for long and painful practice. You must carve a thousand faces, as Michelangelo said, to carve one *good* face.

Initially, it is important to understand your goal and the steps towards it. What kind of face do you want to carve? Is it to be grotesque, caricature, formal face, or portrait (*see* Fig. 12)? Is it to be in the round or in low relief? If you are shooting at formal faces or portraits, endless carving of caricatures, for example, will be of little help. And once you abandon the profile depiction to carve faces at various angles, low-relief carving can be most difficult of all, because actual proportion must be replaced by a simulation of proportion in the third dimension. The smooth, well-rounded cheek may actually become almost angular in cross-section, and eyes and mouth are no longer uniform. The Egyptians, for example, spent centuries learning how to carve a relief head other than in profile.

The head is roughly like an egg set on its point on the neck which is half a head long in front for a male, thinner and longer for a female. The neck is like a tree growing out of the shoulders and leaning forward, so that the head is set forward, more so in the female than in the male. The face—forgetting for the moment any receding hairline—is the length of the hand and about two-thirds as wide as it is high. A most important fact is that the eyes are almost centered vertically—a very common mistake is to place them too high. Each eye is a fifth to a quarter of the width of the head, and they are normally about an eye-width apart. The tip of the nose is about halfway from the center line of the eye to the chin, and the mouth center one-third of the distance from nose tip to chin. Mouth width is 1½ to 2 times eye width, lip thickness (at center) a fifth of the distance from nose to chin. The ears are roughly as long as the nose and aligned with it front to back. They are just behind the center of the skull.

The most common mistake in face carving is to have the cheeks too far

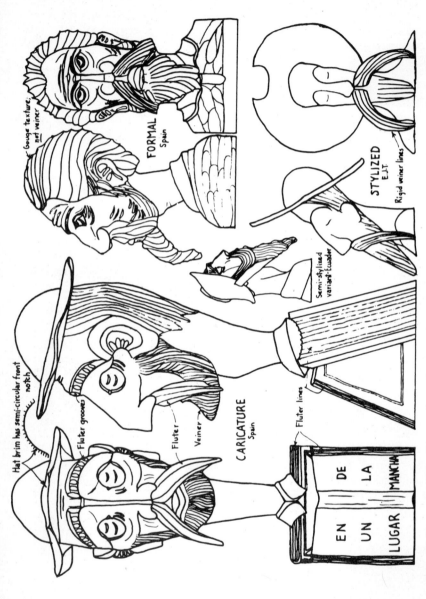

Gouge texture, not veiner

FORMAL
Spain

STYLIZED
E.J.T.
Rigid veiner lines

Semi-stylized
variant-Ecuador

Hat brim has semi-circular front notch

Fluter grooves

Fluter

Veiner

CARICATURE
Spain

Fluter lines

EN
UN
LUGAR

DE
LA
MANCHA

Fig. 12. Four versions of a popular subject, Don Quixote. Compare the simplification, streamlining, and lack of detail of the stylized version (lower right) with the detail of the others, which also put more stress on texturing. See also Figs. 13 and 14.

forward. The angle formed by nose tip and cheekbone is roughly 90° and the nose projects from the egg shape of the head when viewed in profile. The chin also projects from the same viewpoint, but not as much—only the classic witch has chin and nose tip aligned vertically, and even vertical alignment of brow and chin is rare (and makes for a very pugnacious face).

All of these ratios are averages, of course; any face varies from them. That's what makes us individuals. The face is not symmetrical, even if it looks that way; the small differences from side to side account for the abnormal look of a mirror image. Also, hairdos, beards, jowls and fleshiness tend to obliterate the egg shape, so the basic proportions are merely takeóff points for carving. (The Spanish caricature carver capitalized on this by making Don Quixote's face much longer than an egg shape and making Sancho Panza's almost pear-shaped—*see* Figs. 13 and 15.)

To me, there are two vital elements in making an in-the-round head in repose. One is the eye size, shape and positioning; the other the profile,

Figs. 13 and 14. Contemporary Spanish caricature of Don Quixote (left), with somewhat stylized eyes and nose. Formal head of the same subject is rough-finished and tinted, and also from Spain. Hair and beard variations are suggested by gouge cuts rather than the fine veiner lining of the first piece.

which includes brow, mouth and chin. The profile is particularly important in portraiture because it establishes the basic structure of the face to a considerable degree. (Typical profiles belonging to certain races or even tribes are being obliterated by intermarriage, particularly in the United States, so that children today often show decidedly mixed profiles. In countries where there has been a considerable period of such intermarriage, Mexico and Latin America for example, many mestizos are a mixture of Spanish or other European blood and one or more Indian tribes, and their precise origins are almost impossible to establish visually.)

The basic face, whatever its eyes and profile, is distorted by expression. Surprise shoots the eyebrows up, anger pulls them together and down, joy widens the mouth and lifts its outer ends, thus partially closing the lower eyelids, while pique and despair draw mouth corners down (tending to narrow the mouth). The face is also affected by age: vast networks of wrinkles, crow's-feet at eye corners, deep lines around the mouth, hollowing of cheeks,

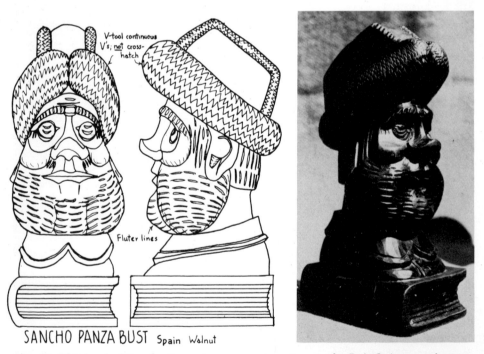

SANCHO PANZA BUST Spain Walnut

Fig. 15. This head of Sancho Panza is a companion-piece to the Don Quixote caricature (Fig. 13), and contrasts sharply with it in that it is stubby where Don Quixote is attenuated. Similarities in eye treatment identify them as products of the same sculptor.

bulging of the nose, possibly greater prominence of the chin from loss of teeth, sagging jowls. It is also affected by corpulence—the fat face is wider in the jowls and has few wrinkles. These are refinements of face carving, but are essential if the face is to be representative and alive, rather than static and frozen.

Fig. 16. Smiling conquistador (left) and dour Scot are two of the four caricatured faces on this four-way head carved in cedar and mounted on onyx. The other heads are Zapotec Indians. Such a carving provides excellent practice for carving faces.

You can practice all these elements by carving a four-way head or two. (*See* Fig. 16.) They're caricatures, of course, but they do place the nose on the corner of a block and the eyes midway of each side (in this case carved flat with the side). Or try a single head, starting with the nose at one corner of a squared stick. This automatically leaves wood for the ears and gives a reasonable slope to the cheeks, an idea which the Mayans used on cornice ends a thousand years ago.

Carve a step-by-step head

START WITH A SQUARED BLOCK. Mark off from one corner, both ways, a line down from the top 1½ times the width of the block; i.e., if the block is 1 in (25.4 mm) square, put the line 1½ in (38.1 mm) down from the top. This is the chin line (Step I, top left, in Fig. 17). Halve the distance from this line to the top and put in the eye line. Now, a third of the way down from nose to chin, put in the mouth line. (Some authorities make this two-fifths of the way; the difference is not too vital.) Now cut in perpendicularly across the corner at the chin and nose lines, and notch out wood from below so that you create a new sloping flat about a fourth the width of a side. Notch the corner at the eye line (Step II), cutting from both above and below. Also mark notch-outs for the ears, the bottom one in line with the bottom of the nose, the upper *above* the eye by an eye width. (It is convenient at this point to draw in a "reference eye" on the eye line, about a third of the block width in length and shaped like the oval of the complete eye, not just of the "open" part between the lids: Step II in sketch.)

Begin to round up the head on top, notching over the ears to make this easier, and splitting off the wood above the eye notch to flatten the brow (Step III). Also notch below the ears and rough-form the neck. Draw in eyebrow lines on the brow as arcs meeting at the center of the eye notch and rising to 1½ eye widths over the eye line at each side. Mark in a nose triangle with its apex in line with the *top* of the eyebrow arcs (so there is some width of nose at the eye line). Cut V-notches along the nose line to meet perpendicular notches cut in along the eyebrow line (also Step III). Mark in the mouth line again, and extend the lines on each side of the nose to the lower edge of the jaw. Cut a small notch to denote the mouth-center line, then cut away the sharp point of the chin and round the chin and mouth area to notches extending down from the nose.

Now begin to rough-shape the eye (Step IV), remembering that the eyeballs and lids are about an eye width apart and that each eye is about a fifth of the finished width of the head. Making these shapes involves deepening the grooves between eye and nose, and carving grooves between brow and eye, and eye and cheek.

This completes rough-forming, and you're ready for the shaping of Step V. Form the eyeball more accurately and slope the line below the brow. (Here we're carving an inset eye. Many people have eyes with folds or laps in this area, but let's leave that for a later head.) Rough-form the nostrils and fair off the cheeks next to them. Draw in a hairline to suit your fancy, then the

Fig. 17. Carving a head, step by step (I to VI).

ears and nose, and carve the shapes. Remember that there is a bulge along the brow line, particularly in males, so slope back from just above the eyebrow line to the hairline. Now you're ready for Step VI, finishing. Final-shape the ears and put in whatever convolutions you wish. Do the same for the nose and nostrils, as well as for the lips and chin. Normally the lower lip is shorter and fuller than the upper, and there is a definite groove between lower lip and chin—the chin is a fat oval bump, actually. Open the eyes by drawing in lid lines and hollowing out—*very* carefully—between them. Drill pupil holes and suggest the outline of the corneas by shallow V-notching. These latter steps determine the personality of the face, so they must be done carefully. Suggestions and ideas for carving the features are given in this chapter, including sketches. Study them! And good luck.

Carving the eyes—fine points

THE EYES are normally just above the median line of the head, but setting them at the median line is fairly accurate. There is an eye width between normal eyes, two eye widths between the pupil centers. There is one open-eye width between eye and eyebrow, and the eyebrow is highest and widest over the outer third of the eye. Eyes may be larger, or smaller, open wider or less, be wide apart or close. The forehead ends in the outer rim of the orbital (brow) circle.

All of these factors must be considered in laying out and carving eyes. Some other factors are sketched. These include: The upper lid normally covers the upper edge of the cornea; the lower lid is at its lower rim or below. (When the eye looks down, the upper lid lowers with it; the lower lid does not. When the eye looks up, the space between the lids is increased and usually the eyebrow is lifted as well.) The upper lid extends over or outside the lower at the outer edge, and the lower outer corner of the upper lid extends below the center of the globe of the eye. The *canthus major*, the eye muscle next to the nose, must be shown if eye shape is to be right. So must the bulge of the cornea and the bulge of the upper lid over it. Eye-cavity position and shape are very important; whether eyes bulge or are recessed, whether the line where brow meets nose is above or below the eye center, and the exact shape of the folds below the upper eyebrow, all are important if a likeness is to be obtained.

Most of the motion in the eyelids is made by the upper lid. In fact, a closed eye looks as if the upper lid had come down to cover the eyeball, an effect accentuated by the upper lashes, which cover the lower. Lowering the upper lid therefore creates a brooding or sleepy look; raising it can suggest, successively, attention, or alarm and fright. In this last emotion, the cornea may practically disappear upward.

A wink is not just a closed eye, unless the winker is an expert. The normal person winks by pulling up the cheek muscle below, so the whole side of the face, including the mouth, is pulled up. The crease between cheek and eye is intensified and the lower lid pushed up. Wrinkles radiate from the eye corners.

I begin an eye by shaping the oval of the eyeball, taking care to make it large enough to include the lids and allowing for any bulge between eye and brow or anything abnormal—like a puff—beneath it. The eyes may actually slope upward or downward slightly at their outer corners, and they may be slightly above or slightly below the normal eye line. (For rough purposes, the eye line is the center of the skull; actually, for most of us the eyes are just a bit above that, the skull center line running along the center of the lower lid.) Once the eyeball is shaped, be sure the eyeballs are roughly parallel with each other, because the eyeballs are basically in line from the side. The brow and the cheek slope back, so the eyeball is nearer the surface of the face at the outer edges.

Now lay out the lines for the upper and lower lids. The upper lid is normally up above center a bit more than the lower lid is below it, and the *canthus major* muscle at the inner edge points slightly downward toward the nose; this is actually a slight extension of the eye oval. Cut along the eyelid lines and bost or ground out wood between them, retaining the curvature of the ball (which isn't a ball but a long oval, as we see it). If you want to be accurate, carve the cornea as a slightly raised circle extending slightly under the upper lid. It is a circular shallow dome about a third of the width of the visible eye. The upper lid has a slight hump over it. Also, the upper lid extends just beyond the lower at the outer edge. In small figures the pupil can be just a hole drilled (again *very* carefully to avoid splitting off wood above and below) deep enough to appear black in normal light. Final shaping of the lids is the last operation, with perhaps a slight accenting of the cornea edge by V-grooving.

There are many simpler ways to make eyes, beginning with the rough V-notch and painted dot of quick caricatures. I have sketched a number of conventions; suit yourself, depending upon figure size and your abilities. If you really want to be meticulous, don't drill the pupil but carve it out, leaving a tiny regular or arcuate triangle at the top to simulate the "glint."

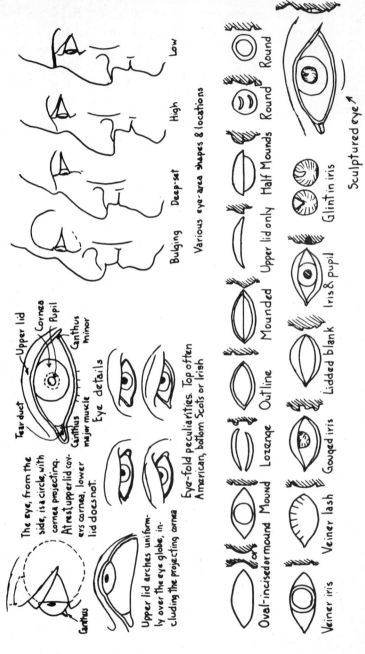

Low

High

Deep-set

Bulging

Various eye-area shapes & locations

The eye, from the side, is a circle, with cornea projecting. At rest, upper lid covers cornea, lower lid does not.

Upper lid
Cornea
Pupil
Canthus minor
Tear duct
Canthus major muscle

Eye details

Eye-fold peculiarities. Top often American, bottom Scots or Irish

Upper lid arches uniformly over the eye globe, including the projecting cornea

Canthus

Oval-incised mound
Mound
Lozenge
Outline
Mounded
Upper lid only
Half Mounds
Round
Round

Veiner lash
Veiner iris
Gouged iris
Liddled blank
Iris & pupil
Glint in iris

Sculptured eye

Fig. 18. Typical eye conventions: upper line simple, lower line more complex.

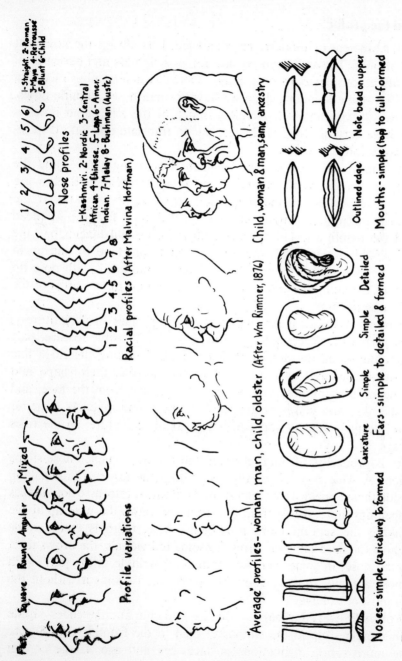

Flat. Square Round Angular Mixed

Profile variations

Nose profiles

1 2 3 4 5 6

1-Straight 2-Roman.
3-Maya 4-Retrousse
5-Blunt 6-Child

1 2 3 4 5 6 7 8

Racial profiles (After Malvina Hoffman)

1-Kashmiri. 2-Nordic 3-Central
African. 4-Chinese. 5-Lapp 6-Amer.
Indian. 7-Malay 8-Bushman (Austr.)

Child, woman & man, same ancestry

Note bead on upper

Outlined edge

Mouths - simple (top) to full-formed

"Average" profiles - woman, man, child, oldster (After Wm Rimmer, 1874)

Caricature Simple Simple Detailed

Ears - simple to detailed & formed

Noses - simple (caricature) to formed

Fig. 19. Profiles and facial variations.

33

The nose and the profile

WHEN STATUES, ancient or modern, are damaged, it is always the nose that bears the brunt of it. The same can be said for prizefighters and caricatures. The nose is often considered to be a major factor in determining race and disposition. Nose shape is inherited, so we have Roman noses, Semitic noses, retroussé noses . . . you name it. Actually, much of the lore about noses is untrue. They have certain physical shapes, but to translate that into disposition and the like is folly.

Be that as it may, the nose is a key element in carving a face, and the shape it is given can be vital. Actually, the nose, forehead and chin are interrelated, and are based on the shape and structure of the skull. If the skull is rounded in front, the nose tends to be wide and flat, the forehead receding, and the mouth and chin profile both receding and longer than the norm. If the skull is squared off, the forehead and chin tend to line up in profile and we get the classic relationship of eyes at mid-head, with nose tip halfway down to the chin, and mouth centerline one-third to two-fifths of the distance from nose to chin.

The effect of all this is to make the nose very important in portraiture—more so than perhaps it deserves to be. But it is a very visible feature, particularly in profile, so all the details must be right, including the ridge line and overall height, as well as the spread of the nostrils, their shape and inclination, the meeting of nose and brow, its projection from the face, and so on. Miss the nose and you miss the portrait, and no mistake. As a matter of fact, make the nose genteel and you have a poor caricature, so the rules work both ways.

Nose width is primarily a frontal element, but it does influence nose shape and projection. A wide nose is usually flat, tilting the nostrils and making the flesh outside them appear wider than from the front. A retroussé nose makes the nostril openings more visible from the front and raises the nose tip above its base, making the septum more prominent. Also, there is considerable variation in how the nose joins the brow. In some individuals, the brows meet in a V over the nose; in some there is a transverse wrinkle at the joining; in others, the nose actually runs up above the brow line or joins it without the declivity that most of us have.

The swell of puffy eyes, the shape of the lips and chin and the cheek profile are all much more visible in the silhouette than in the frontal view. So are many of the more subtle distinctions of race, sex and age. If the correct

34

profile is achieved in a carving, much of the frontal forming of lips, chin and nose is simplified. Thus it pays to study the various profiles in which I have tried to show the variations, and perhaps have over-emphasized them slightly (Fig. 19).

The nose itself can be a simple tapered wedge in quick studies, but can be very detailed in faces expressing a particular emotion, or in a portrait. Even more important, however, in portraiture or emotion is the mouth, which actually is the biggest single element in expression. It is changed in shape to express an emotion, and the rest of the face must accommodate itself. Also, we have come to associate full lips with sensuousness, thin lips with severity, restraint, even parsimony. The mucous portions of a full mouth may occupy as much as two-fifths of the total distance from nose base to chin, particularly in female faces. The female is customarily carved with thicker lips than the male, perhaps because we have become accustomed to artificial widening if the lips are too thin. (Paradoxically, the brutish male face also has thicker, more protruding lips.) The hearty laugh is supposed to show teeth—which adds a carving problem. And so it goes.

There are an endless number of details about carving the mouth, including the amount of cupid's bow in the upper lip, the comparative "pouting" fullness of the lower lip, the groove from upper-lip center to septum, whether or not to carve a bead along the top of the upper lip. (It is very rare in nature, but even the Egyptians knew it enhanced the face of Queen Nefertiti.) I always seem to have trouble with the subtle curves at the end of the mouth, and between it and the chin, because a slight change alters the expression so much.

The ears, once the amount of projection has been established, are basically also a matter of the silhouette. Many carvers give them a fairly standardized shape, with a few token gouge lines to suggest the convolutions inside. I have drawn, and usually carve, a somewhat more exact shape, because it is quite visible in the full head. Also, the jaw line comes up to meet the middle of the ear lobe. It can be quite prominent in a square-jawed male, almost indistinguishable in a soft-faced female, and shape varies widely with individuals. But it does establish the beginning of the neck, and the position of the Adam's apple in male necks with prominent ones. It also establishes the thinning of the head bulge behind the ears, which in turn has to do with the shaping of the back of the head. It must always be kept in mind, even when you carve a bushy-haired and bearded head.

Portrait faces

To MAKE A PORTRAIT—or a caricature—of an individual, you must identify and catalog the features that are unusual or abnormal, even if only slightly so. This is relatively easy with some individuals—witness the distinctive hair styles and moustaches of Hitler and Charlie Chaplin, the big ears of Clark Gable, the craggy face and mole of Lincoln, the square jaw and mouth of Washington (caused, I am told, by poorly fitted false teeth made of wood), the bushy hair and youthful face of Kennedy, the toothy grin of Carter, the specially shaped and prominent noses of Durante, Nixon, and Hope. Only when a face is near the norm—as in the case of Gerald Ford—is there a problem.

The men I mentioned above are public figures and have been cartooned so often that the eccentricities of their faces are well known. The cartoonist and the caricaturist accentuate these eccentricities, of course, but often so does the portraitist, although his accentuation is more subtle. Indeed, the line between portrait and caricature may be very hazy—one may be produced when the other is intended. I have a life-size portrait of myself in oil that my wife has never hung because the artist crossed that hazy line—at least in her opinion.

Some of us seem to have been born with the ability to distinguish and depict subtle differences in countenances. This is true of most portrait artists; the rest of us can approach portraiture only with much effort, time and difficulty. Also, the portrait artist seems to get some of the personality, the inner feelings, of his subject into his rendering. It may be a special position of the head, a quirk of an eyebrow or the lips, a "look" around the eyes. This is especially difficult to accomplish in wood because the material is solid and opaque, while flesh may vary subtly in tint or tone, even, occasionally, in translucence. Also, it is difficult in sculpture to reproduce the eye, to distinguish between pupil and iris, as well as to show the paleness of the eyeball around the iris, and the color and density of the eyelashes.

Another difficulty is to express the fleeting expression caused by muscle movement and the interrelationship of muscle, bone and skin. This is particularly hard when the subject is a child or a fleshy adult, because of the absence of the lines and wrinkles that personalize a mature face. In my own limited efforts at portraiture these elements have caused extreme difficulty, so it is with complete bewilderment that I watch portraitists capture a likeness. They have an inner "eye" which I do not, apparently, possess. I have had some success in working from photographs, which "freeze" an expression, particularly when they include strong light and shadow. (The usual frontal flash photos are almost useless because they flatten shadows.)

Portraitists have told me that they look for and record, either mentally or by quick sketches, the slight abnormalities we've been talking about, and then exaggerate them slightly in producing the portrait. It can be a lengthy process of trial and error, which is difficult when the base material is wood. Even the meticulous transfer of physical dimensions may not work, particularly if the wood has grain or imperfections, or is difficult to carve. This suggests walnut or mahogany, or teak if you can get it, all of which have enough inherent color to create an initial disadvantage. Maple and holly are better for color, but much more difficult to work. Pine or basswood are scarcely worth the time for anything but a quick caricature supported by tinting. And texturing—the development of tiny flat planes or an overall roughened surface, which delights the sculptor in clay and gives his work a personal touch—is doubly difficult in wood because such effects are usually obtained by appliquéing more base material upon an already well-sculptured likeness, and the woodcarver can't put material back that he has already cut away. All in all, if you attempt portraiture, I wish you luck. You'll need that, as well as skill and patience—both for yourself and your subject—because a fairly sure way of losing any likeness you may have achieved is to fiddle with it in the absence of the subject.

CHAPTER V

Carve a Caricature

Some types are standard, some are unique, but the viewer should smile

CARICATURES have undoubtedly brought pleasure and enjoyment to more people than formal carvings, whether it be to the carver or to the recipient. Until very recently, caricature has not been recognized as an art form because it violates a great many of the principles of formal art. Now it is an acknowledged folk art. Items can be made rapidly, thus sell at popular prices for the most part, and the quality does not have to meet some traditional standard. While we tend to think of caricature and whittling as knife products, caricaturists in Europe are much more likely to use chisels—because they have learned to carve that way. And American caricaturists with considerable experience supplement the knife with small gouges like the veiner and the fluter because they're so much faster and more convenient in producing concavities and fine lines.

Not all so-called caricatures *are* caricatures, of course; some are simply crude and some result from mistakes; some are simple and some quite sophisticated; some are original, while many are copies of traditional patterns. The line between realism and caricature is ill defined and. caricature is often an unintended result. The carver is seeking to achieve more than a frozen, stick-like figure, or to suggest an emotion or idea that goes beyond physical characteristics. He must do this by providing expression, or by exaggerating a pose or physical characteristic, which is what an artist does when he achieves a portrait that is somewhat beyond a photograph of the subject. Over-exaggeration makes a likeness into a caricature, but where the line between them is, no one can say exactly.

Scandinavian carvers have for many years produced angular, blocky figures that are very well done. They are almost formulaic: three creases at elbow and knee, saggy breeches, wrinkled coats, slightly battered hats. Tyrolean carvers produce rounded, chubby figures. African carvers produced lampoons of the white men and women who bought them; these tended to attenuation, as do modern Haitian ones. Most of them show the subject with a smile or a grin, in many cases self-deprecating because of the smiler's dilapidated condition. We have developed a style similar to the Scandinavian in our so-called "Western," "mountain," or "Ozark" caricatures. The subjects are cowboys and Indians, tramps or workmen, but the stump or over-thin figure, the ill-fitting clothes and the V-notch wrinkles are characteristic. Better figures have strong planes, light or no tinting, and some emotion expressed in faces which are generated with relatively few lines.

In my first book, published over 40 years ago, I pictured an Italian band and provided the pattern for one member. Recently, a reader asked for patterns of the other members—he likes the band better than anything I've since provided, which is about 2,500 designs! (And these band figures are no longer carved in the Tyrol.) Just in case there are others who feel the same way, the original band is pictured here, with the patterns this time (Fig. 20). I have also included five caricatures from an unusual (at least to me) Scandinavian source, Denmark (Figs. 21 and 22). There are also two of a great series of figures being carved by a Michigan retiree in Florida, E. Kjellstrom, obviously of Scandinavian extraction (Fig. 23). He produces these at a rate of four a day, against standing orders. Most are male, seated or standing, with the characteristic face, and many have painted-on elements, such as the small picture on the breast of the birdwatcher, or the miniscule eyelashes on both. Mr. Kjellstrom is a skilled painter as well as a whittler. His designs can be carved rapidly with just the knife. Most are painted, but this is unnecessary because the blocky figure, detail, and strong lines will carry the carving. The figure is readily adaptable to whatever "props" the carver plans for that particular subject, and is unusual because of elements like the chair for the seated figure and the painting on the chest of the birdwatcher. (Elements like the bird, binoculars, and chair are carved separately and assembled, of course.)

Caricature carvers also tend to use themselves as models for facial expression—probably via a mirror—so the faces of their carvings tend to be their own, caricatured. (One American caricaturist, of Italian descent, makes a wide variety of caricatures, but all have his own distinctively shaped head and face, rounded like an olive, and all are sanded and rounded in finishing, like many Italian carvings.)

For contrast, I have included a jaeger (hunter) head from Oberammergau (Fig. 26). Compare the sophistication and detail of this carving with the simplicity of the others. This is *not* a caricature, but a study of an individual

Fig. 20. This street orchestra was commonly produced in the Tyrol of Austria about 50 years ago. The figures are tinted and stand about 6 in (15 cm) high.

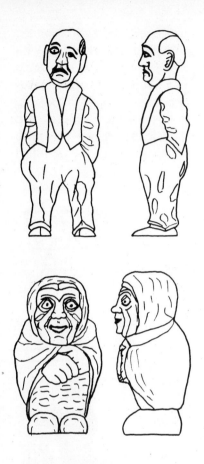

Fig. 21. These two Danish caricatures border on the grotesque. Note the strong lines and planes, the oversized heads, the droll expressions.

that shows his personality without lampooning him, yet it still expresses the humor for which a caricature strives. It is probably produced almost as swiftly as the cruder figures, but by a professional who has had extensive training, not only in carving but in anatomy as well, and who uses gouges to obtain subtle concavities. Compare this particularly with the chimney sweep caricature and the seated couple from Denmark (Fig. 22), which have almost no modelling and relatively little detail, or even with Kjellstrom's figures, which have both carved and painted detail, yet appear primitive by comparison. The step from primitive to formal can be a very long one.

Slight variations in arm and hand positions make it possible for the same basic caricature to be engaged in a variety of pursuits, depending upon what is placed in the hand or how the figure is dressed. This can vastly reduce the amount of design and roughing time for a particular figure. Mr. Kjellstrom does this, as do many caricaturists who turn out figures of professionals: doctors, dentists, lawyers, or whatever. Also, certain faces are identified with certain individuals, as witness the Don Quixote and Sancho Panza visages shown here (Figs. 24 and 25) and in the preceding chapter on carving faces (Figs. 12–15.). I have sketched seven different caricatures of Don Quixote taken from five different countries (Fig. 25), some designs as much as a hundred years old, yet all the Quixote faces are thin and drawn and have the drooping moustachios and the goatee. Sancho Panza is always identified

Fig. 22. Three old Danish caricatures of country people include a seated couple and a chimney sweep. Such figures were formerly carved by farmers as a wintertime occupation, and were usually colored with dull tints.

by a fatter, peasant face, usually with short moustache and beard and a hat on the back of the head. As can be seen from the sketches of Quixote, he can be wearing or carrying one of three kinds of hat, be in full or partial armor and armed in various ways, but the hat designs, the doublet or breast-plate, and the stripes around the upper legs are always the same——established by tradition. The same can (and has) been said about other historical figures, particularly if we have no precise portrait of them.

Fig. 23. Two basic figures, one seated, one standing, are hand-tinted and have painted additions, like that on the bird watcher's jacket. They are Scandinavian in form, and were carved by E. Kjellstrom, of Florida.

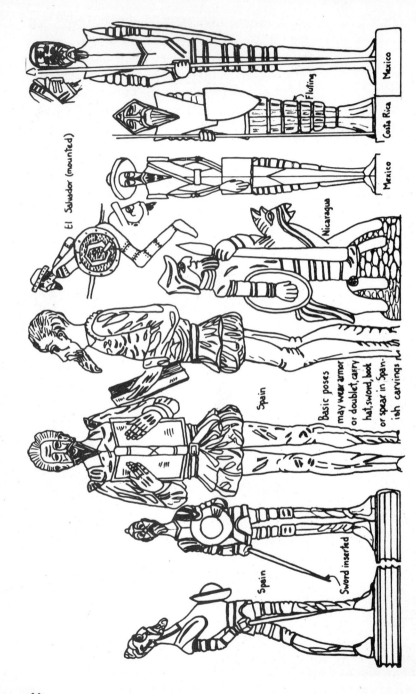

Fig. 24. Seven caricatures of Don Quixote, from five different countries, are sketched. Some of these figures are 100 years old.

SANCHO PANZA
Spain

Fig. 25. Don Quixote and Sancho Panza are the basic caricature subjects in Spanish-speaking countries. They are carved in endless variations, and their costumes and hand props vary as well.

Fig. 26. This small head of a jaeger (or huntsman) is very intricate, and is more of a portrait than a caricature. It was carved in Oberammergau and its back is flat, so it can be hung or mounted on a wall.

45

Fig. 27. This bass viol player is in jelutong and is a caricature of a friend. Personalizing inanimate objects is a common form of caricature and can be quite challenging.

It is possible to personalize an object in order to create a character from a particular calling or to suggest a personal characteristic. Thus, an identifiable caricatured human face can be put on the body of an animal or drawn within the outlines of an object such as a kettle, a pot, a bottle, or whatever. One example of this kind of caricature is the bass-fiddle player I carved in jelutong (Fig. 27). In point of fact, the possibilities in caricature are almost endless and there is little reason to repeat the same one, unless it is done for commercial reasons, as in the case of poor old Don Quixote.

CHAPTER VI

Who Took the "A" Train?

An assembly of various caricatures in various woods

MANY COMPLEX CARVINGS are made in parts and then assembled, for a variety of reasons. Individual figures made this way take advantage of grain, save wood, reduce the danger of checking. Also, these days it is hard to find large blocks of good wood, so large forms must of necessity be built up. Many carvers are basically whittlers who use the knife principally, and work best with relatively small pieces. This has led to the assembled carving, usually with each figure, or part of it, whittled individually. The so-called "Western-style" carvings are a good example: figures are assembled in a poker game, barroom, store, farrier's shed, ranch scene or other suitable background. Often, every detail is meticulously reproduced, even to the rungs on chairs and labels on miniature bottles, pips on cards, and all the rest. There are also adjustable assemblies in which a group of figures is included, but each figure can be placed separately at the whim of the owner. Examples of this are the Noah's ark, the Nativity scene, and, to stretch the definition a bit, the chessboard.

The virtue, and the complication, of such assemblies is that they can and should be viewed from many angles, so that they must be displayed, in most instances, on a pedestal in the open. I found that certain of my three-dimensional sculptures, like four-way and 12-way heads, a column of dolphins and the like, were constantly being picked up by viewers, so I customarily display them on a lazy Suzan—or even build one in if the figure is large enough. Such a carving is like a mobile in that it can present a great many separate "pictures," depending upon the viewing angle. This suggests carvings made like children's blocks, in which a scene may be varied by the way the blocks are stacked or placed. Figures might even have standard sides which could mate or interlock in the manner of a jigsaw puzzle.

These thoughts led me to the idea of a group of free-standing individuals which might be arranged in various ways, as they might occur in nature. I

Fig. 28. Mother with child and bundles is in cedar; Puerto Rican messenger with radio to his ear is in pecan. She sits on a nonexistent seat; he grips a nonexistent pole.

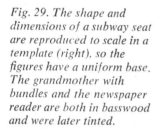

Fig. 29. The shape and dimensions of a subway seat are reproduced to scale in a template (right), so the figures have a uniform base. The grandmother with bundles and the newspaper reader are both in basswood and were later tinted.

Fig. 30. Two more standing figures: a portly businessman in mahogany and a black "dude" in walnut, with a separate birch cane whittled from a tongue depresser. The "dude" is leaning against an imaginary door.

48

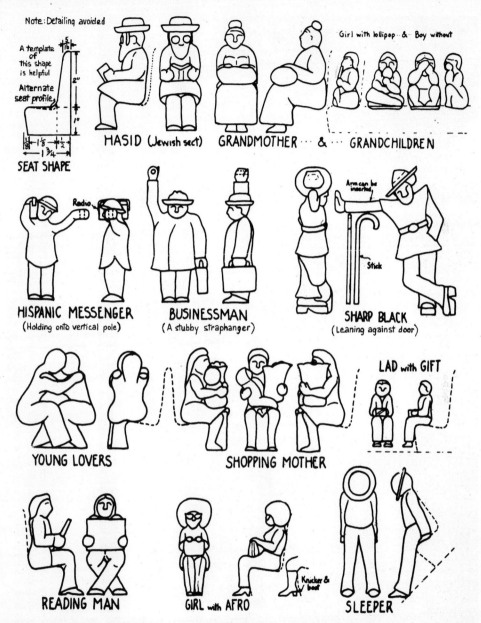

Fig. 31. Sketches of all the passengers, and of the seat template (top left).

Fig. 32. Near-faceless figures ride a non-existent subway car in this 13-figure group mounted on a 5×17-in (12.5×42.5-cm) cherry base. This piece provides good practice in whittling various woods and posing the human body. Similar figures can form other assemblies.

began with the idea of buildings of various shapes and sizes—a miniature village. Then I somehow got into the variety of people who take public transportation, their differences in life style, mode of dress, attitude, and all the rest. This led me, in turn, to a New York phenomenon—the subway, and the various characters who populate it at any time. (It might just as well have been a bus, a waiting room, a park.) Perhaps the greatest variation is on trains running up to Harlem and the Bronx, which include individuals of all races, ages, social levels, dimensions, and intentions. Thus began my "A Train," with a name borrowed from a Duke Ellington composition. It also appealed to me because I could use several varieties of wood, and because each figure could be a microcosm of humanity, intent upon his or her own pursuits and unrelated to other people on the train except by the coincidence of their being in the same place at the same time. (Authors have used this device for years in novels dealing with a disaster or important event.)

To begin with, the hardened subway rider scarcely notices other people—he is too preoccupied with his own problems, so he yields or pushes his way without conscious thought and his view of other people is hazy, at best. Therefore, I decided not to detail the features of the individuals or to carve much detail into their garb, but to concentrate on types and poses. Originally, I planned to have the figures seated in a row, but most subways have standees, leaners and sprawlers as well, so, as I made such figures, I found myself being pushed into a detailed background which, for me, would spoil the whole idea because there is a great deal of physical detail in a subway car (as there is in a bar, for example). This tends to take over, so that the viewer has difficulty focusing on the center of interest. First, I decided to simply have the seat, then I subtracted the back of the seat, eventually got rid of the seat and all detail; the background must be imagined.

It may be surprising for some carvers to learn that no one seems to have difficulty realizing that this is a scene in a subway car (or another kind of commuter transport somewhere else, although the characters elsewhere would probably be different), and the absence of a concrete "support"—or background—adds to the intrigue of the work.

I made the first several figures of basswood, assuming darker woods for the others, but, on assembly, I found that the white was too garish in contrast, so it was necessary to tone it; I used the German Beiz finishes (#1611 and #1614), which provide a greyed yellow or tan, darker in the indentations. The tall black is of walnut (Fig. 30), the straphanger of red mahogany, the woman with bundles is in cedar (Fig. 28), the messenger is of pecan

(Fig. 28), and the girl with the Afro is of butternut. Finish is Danish wood oil, which contains a little wax. The base is cherry and the figures are both glued and nailed to it with headless brads. Brads are also used to reinforce figures where they meet each other, so the assembly is no longer adjustable.

Most of these figures can be sawed out of wood that is 1⅝ in (4.2 cm) thick as planed. Because they are small, and because details of face and hands are not included (at least in mine), they can be whittled quite rapidly. The difficulty lies in avoiding over-precision and unnecessary detail. Unfortunately, people just don't see much detail in a subway car, and the carving should reflect that fact—it should be an accurate picture as a whole, not an assembly of accurate details.

To carry out the idea of undetailed figures, I left knife marks on the pieces and no finishing beyond that of the knife itself—no sanding or rasping or gouging of detail. I did, however, drill the straphanger's hand for the non-existent strap and the messenger's hand for the non-existent pole, and I provided all the figures with the hand props they would probably be carrying: radio, cane, bundles, lollipop, book, newspaper, glasses. These are as much a part of the individual as clothes. The figures are single pieces, except for the leaner, whose out thrust arm is set into a drilled hole, thus saving a considerable amount of good wood. Also, his cane is whittled from birch (a tongue depressor) and stained.

The base is ½-in (12.7-mm) cherry, 5¼ × 17¼ in (13.4 × 43.8 cm). There is no rigid requirement for this—it just happens to hold the figures in the order I chose. I was attempting contrasts: Hasid versus hippie, sprawling figure versus "all-business" man, and so on. Also, I assumed a central cross-bench to shorten the overall length; the group spread along one long seat is a bit too long. This leaves the children projecting interestingly in air, each being attached to the adjacent figure by glue and pin. (The two children, incidentally, were carved from a scrap of the grandmother, split in two.)

It still would be interesting to leave the figures so that they could be moved and rearranged, but that would require a real seat, perhaps even a real background, and the eventual arrangement turned out to be more fun, in my opinion, than the original idea.

CHAPTER VII

As We Carve Ourselves (Native Figures)

AMONG PRIMITIVE PEOPLES, the more imaginative carvers produce figures of their gods and the elements; the less imaginative produce miniatures of the familiar things around them. Among more sophisticated carvers, the highly skilled make figures of people; those less adept make figures of animals or objects. These are generalizations, of course, and do not always hold true. Regardless of skill, some of us are compelled, by ambition and competition, to attempt subjects that are well beyond us, and the result may be disproportion and unintended caricature. If someone is overweight, we carve him fat; if he has big ears or a big nose, we enlarge them or it. We produce, in effect, stereotypes—that is, caricatures or cartoons, whether we want to or not.

This is particularly true when someone attempts a portrait of an animal, or of a person of another race; we do not see the subtle differences which we distinguish in people "like us." All blacks, for example, do not have broad noses and thick lips; all Germans are not fat with close-cropped hair; Indians are not red, nor are Orientals slant-eyed. The fact is that the true racial or tribal figure is disappearing, so we must go back into the past to produce it.

It is only natural that any carver will picture local subjects; they are the most familiar. Mechanical and physical objects are measurable, animals and people much less so. Thus we rely on costume or environment to suggest identity. Western carvers do cowboys and Indians; Midwestern carvers do farmers, hunters or trappers; Eastern carvers make fishermen—all more recognizable by their garb and tools than by their faces (which are usually standard "American," lean and lined).

This is not an American peculiarity—carvers of other nations do the same thing. They too get some of the racial or tribal characteristics of their neighbors into their work, but they rely upon costume or appurtenances to distinguish occupation or geographical location. More important, any figure of a foreigner or of a person of another race we or they produce is likely to be a caricature.

In this chapter I have gathered together several examples from a number of countries to illustrate these points. All but two were produced by native carvers and they range from the simplest sort of depiction, like the Nicaraguan Indians (Fig. 33), to a sophisticated and stylized rendition of a Haitian woman (Fig. 34). They have one thing in common: they were produced for a regional likeness rather than for a price, so the work is painstaking. There are some caricatures, as well as more formal treatments. Among the group, there are surprisingly good renditions of two Chinese (Fig. 37); the carvers somehow caught a better likeness of their neighbors than did the other artists—at least in my opinion.

Some notes may be of interest. The man with the hand ax (Fig. 36) is from Spain and is not a crisp-edged carving but one in which the edges have been rounded intentionally. The lines of his clothes are accentuated by trenching along them (double lines in the sketch), and the entire figure is stained dark and brought to a gloss. The gloss and the rounding tend to defeat the carver's purpose, in my opinion, making the figure look like molded plastic. It is, however, a sturdy figure, a good pose, and shows more accurate observation, and more life, than the Zinconteco man from southern Mexico (Fig. 35). Each is carved from one piece of wood. In the Zinconteco figure, the carver has resurrected the large flat hat with many gaily colored ribbons (after a man marries, the number and brightness of the ribbons rapidly diminish), over-the-shoulder bag, scarf, distinctive huaraches, and shorts. (Nowadays, men of the tribe wear jeans, as do the men of another tribe in the area, who formerly wore loincloths done like a baby's diaper.)

Another Mexican excursion into the past is La Malinche (Fig. 38), by an Indian in San Martín Tilcajete, near Oaxaca, who drew almost entirely upon his imagination. She was a coastal Indian from far away, near Vera Cruz. (She was Cortez' mistress and interpreter.) This is a large figure, made for a gable decoration, 15½ in (39.4 cm) tall and painted in colors. She was, in a sense, a traitor to her own people, so the carver gave her a distorted, slightly hairy chin. He also provided modern dress coupled with an old elaborate headdress and rattles.

Also from Mexico is the figure of the rebel (Fig. 39)—a standard bearded face which could be Spanish or even Nordic (except for the cedar color). He is identifiable only by his dress and accoutrements. I have also included two of my own figures of Mexicans (Figs. 41 and 42), one of a woman offering a gift, the other a caricatured head. The woman praying is in holly and might well be an American—except that she is on her knees, wearing a shawl and offering a bowl. I carved the caricatured head from a piece of cedar bedpost, principally to practice the carving of rings—in nose, ears and around the clubbed hair. Rather idly, I made the nose an overly large Mayan shape and gave the figure the large and intense eyes of that race. It was not intended as a portrait at all, but my host immediately identified it as a likeness

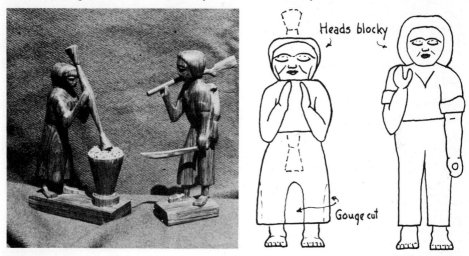

Fig. 33. *A rural couple, carved by a Nicaraguan Indian, is in mahogany and about 5 in (12.5 cm) tall.*

Fig. 34. *This stylized mahogany head is 15 in (37.5 cm) high. It emphasizes the Negroid features and is topped by a distinctive Haitian hairdo.*

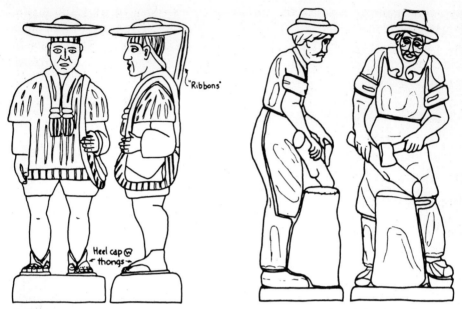

Figs. 35 and 36. A conventional cedar figure of a Zinconteco Indian (left), from the state of Chiapas in southern Mexico, is identifiable by his clothes. The figure of a carver or carpenter "axing a blank" is an older Spanish design, but shows professional skill and has a special finish.

of Benito Juarez, not realizing that it was at least as much a portrait of him, for he comes from the same Zapotec stock. (Neither, by the way, would be caught dead with earrings or clubbed hair.) The final Mexican example (Fig. 40) is a pleasant sun statue which I had to sketch without the use of a photograph. It is a delightful and imaginative composition, but exchange the rays for a robe and cowl and the figure becomes that of a monk.

The Haitian figures offer a sharp contrast to these diverse Mexican ones, particularly in their sophistication. Woodcarving is much more important in the Haitian economy than in the Mexican, which may account for this to a degree. Haitians have been exposed to French rather than Spanish influence, and to tourists, much more than have Mexican Indians. Oldest in style of the Haitian carvings, and probably the most truly local, is the itinerant (Fig. 45), identifiable by the stick and bundle which our own tramps used to carry as well. He has an excellent and sympathetically rendered face, so one feels he is likeable and human. Contrast him with the rather typical American carving of the "Old Timer" (Fig. 44).

Figs. 37 and 38. Two Chinese ivory miniatures (above), about 3 in (7.5 cm) tall. La Malinche (right), mistress of Cortes, was carved in Oaxaca. She is of copal, tinted, and 15½ in (29cm) tall.

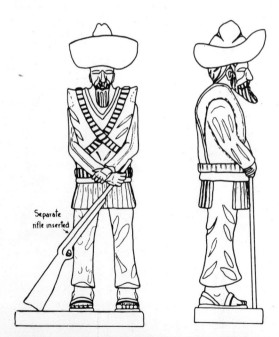

Separate rifle inserted

Fig. 39. This bearded rebel, 10 in (25 cm) high, is in cedar and is identifiable by his "uniform."

The male and female busts (Fig. 46) on bookends are "standards"—less personalized renderings of typical Haitians. They contrast rather sharply with the caricatured figures of the man and woman (Fig. 43), and with the highly stylized female head. These latter three all exaggerate the Haitian Negro's facial characteristics, in one case with a humorous, in the other with an

Figs. 40 and 41. Mexican sun statue (left) is 2 ft (60 cm) tall. The kneeling woman in American holly is identifiable by her pose, her shawl, and her offering, all of which suggests a Central American derivation.

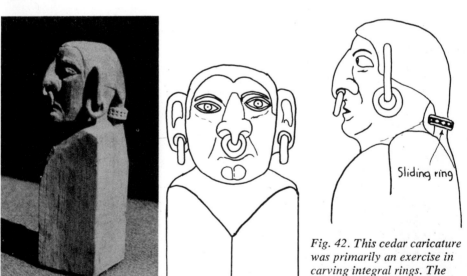

Fig. 42. This cedar caricature was primarily an exercise in carving integral rings. The features are Zapotec, hence beak-nosed and fierce-eyed.

understanding, hand. The caricatures were knocked out in short order, and to order; the others are much more deliberate and careful carvings. Detailing on the busts is particularly fine (as it is on the itinerant) and shows professional skill. The stylized girl has hair textured with small random gouge cuts and built into a bound pyramid; a variation curls the hair up into a high cornucopia. All of these figures, by the way, are in mahogany and finished with a low-gloss polish. The caricatures, by contrast, are in primavera (so-called "white mahogany") and finished with a shellac and alcohol mixture, or the equivalent, which gives an objectionable high gloss. The carver also used mahogany stain for color effects—and gets a cheapened look as a result.

Fig. 43. This caricatured couple, about 18 in (45 cm) high, is from Haiti and carved in primavera, stained for skin color. Their faces are individual, not standardized.

(The "Masonic" emblem on the baseball hat is startling, until one discovers that it is also a voodoo symbol.)

Even more sophisticated, and perhaps the result of more generations of fine carving, are the two Chinese ivories. At first glance they look alike and appear undeniably and typically Chinese. However, not only are the poses quite different (in the same general bulk), but so are the costumes and the accoutrements—and, most importantly, the faces. These are caricatures, too, but sophisticated ones. The faces are those of individuals rather than of types. Each is, in its own way, a little masterpiece.

Figs. 44-46. "Old Timer" (above left), an 8-in (20-cm) American figure in maple, suggests a Midwestern farmer. The musing figure of an itinerant (above, center and right), from Haiti, is in ebony and 20 in (50 cm) tall. The mahogany busts (lower left) have typical Haitian features, but are skilled portraits nonetheless, and make delightful bookends.

CHAPTER VIII

The South American Approach

IN SOUTH AMERICA, as on other continents, there are concentrations of wood-carvers. The largest, at present, is in a contiguous three-country area: southern Ecuador, northern Peru (which not too long ago was southern Ecuador, as the Tyrol was once part of Austria), and western Bolivia. This is a high-altitude, wooded region. Carvings, regardless of the country of origin, are generally similar in type and subject, well formed and well rounded, smoothly finished (in contrast, for example, with those of Argentina, which tend to be angular, rougher in finish and stained a fairly uniform black). These are not primitive carvings—they are obviously made by skilled carvers to familiar patterns and are designed for sale to tourists.

Ecuador is by far the most prolific producer of these carvings, with a wide range of both three-dimensional figures and panels, as well as a wide range of subject matter, from religious figures to animals, particularly the llama. Mahogany seems to be the preferred wood. There is evidence of a kind of mass production: the same figure will be available in several sizes, with larger sizes showing more detail. Exact duplication of form and detail suggests profiler roughing, although sellers insist this is not so.

Peruvian carvings are less regular and include a number of individual pieces made by Amazon Indians and other remote tribes. There is less of the Spanish and church influence in the work there, and still less in Bolivia, where favorite subjects appear to be the Indians themselves, although the technique and finish suggest considerable training and direction atop inherent skill. The Argentinean figures, on the other hand, lean heavily to gauchos and horses, but each figure differs in pose and other details from its fellows. In Chile, there is relatively little woodcarving, probably because much of the country is treeless or nearly so. The emphasis appears to be on the carving of other materials, except on Easter Island, which is Chilean only by agreement and treaty.

Most interesting of the carvings shown here, at least to me, are the Bolivian Indian busts (Fig. 47). They have similarly "fierce" faces, but they are

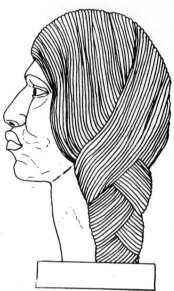

Fig. 47. These male and female heads of Bolivian Indians offer interesting contrasts despite having the same basic look. Note the wider eyebrows and thicker lips of the woman, and the prominent Adam's apple and stronger neck of the male, for example.

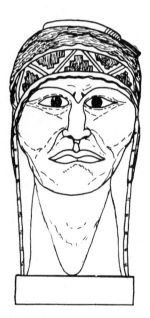

precise in facial detail, and I have tried to point out in my sketches some of the elements that distinguish the feminine head and face from the masculine one. They are superficially alike, but the subtle differences between the sexes are quite clear upon close inspection. How many times have you carved a face that somehow was of the wrong sex? (The cop-out is of course to put on a moustache or beard, or to rely upon the difference in hairdo to distinguish between them, but that's not sure-fire either.)

The Ecuadorian carvers do particularly well with a variety of traveller or mendicant figures. Three are shown (Figs. 48 and 49), each about 8 in (20 cm) tall with base, and made of the same dense medium-brown wood. Each is portrayed with an over-the-shoulder bag and two have begging bowls; all have a plaintive look about the face. The two shown together, however, were bought in Peru (and are officially from what has become northern Peru), while I bought the third (the hatless one) in Spain in a top-quality Madrid shop that preferred these imports to Spanish products. A somewhat similar figure is the piper from Bolivia (Fig. 50), again with the rather fierce face of the Andean Indian and the characteristic cap.

Fig. 48. Two Ecuadorian travellers, or mendicants, reveal an extreme attention to detail on the part of the carver. They seem overburdened and display a pleading look that was obtained by slightly tilting the head and making the eyes heavy-lidded.

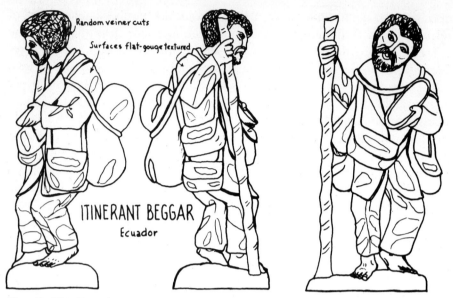

Random veiner cuts

Surfaces flat-gouge textured

ITINERANT BEGGAR
Ecuador

Fig. 49. This Ecuadorian mendicant was found in an exclusive Madrid shop. Note the details of the shoulder-load and begging bowl, features common to the other mendicants as well.

Knitted cap is usual for
Indian men in the Andes

V neckline

Fig. 50. The Indian piper from Bolivia is a basic figure without crease lines in the costumes and other "standards"; he was kept simple to focus attention on the pipes.

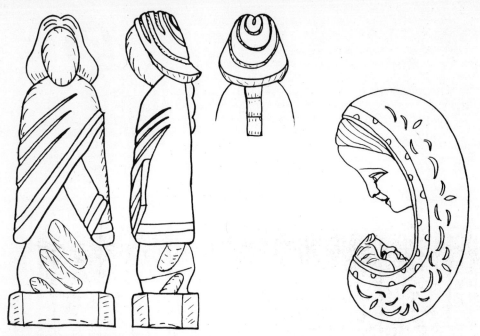

Figs. 51 and 52. The faceless, highly stylized girl (left) is, surprisingly, from Ecuador, as is "Madonna and Child," a simple treatment that is carved both left- and right-handed to be mounted in pairs.

Fig. 53. Caricature of Don Quixote is not a direct copy of Spanish versions. This one is from Ecuador and has a flow and unity that many caricatures often lack.

GAUCHO & GAUCHO BUST Argentine

GAUCHO & PONY
Argentine

Gauchos stained
black & antiqued

Hat separate.

COWBOY
Peru 150 yrs old
Originally painted

HUASO (Cowboy) Chile

Primitive...
carved by a
huaso

Fig. 54. South American versions of cowboys: "gaucho" in Argentina, "huaso" in Chile. They are unpretentious and powerful, and often primitive in design. See also Figs. 55, 56, and 57.

Figs. 55-57. The Argentine gaucho (left) is an obviously self-sufficient individual. The cowboy (center) was carved in Peru 150 years ago. The Brazilian cowboy is actually a modern copy, made from crude wood patterns and cast in rubber.

A number of designs in Ecuador were of the stylized sort, but they seem to be losing favor nowadays. A typical example is the girl with a simple oval replacing the features and a few major lines cut in the skirt and shawl (Fig. 51). She is in sharp contrast to the other figures and to the Madonna and Child panel (Fig. 52). The latter, about 4 in (100 cm) high, is made both left- and right-handed and meant to be used as a wall decoration. (Somewhat smaller ones are produced in Guatemala for pendants.)

Every Spanish-speaking country seems to have adopted Don Quixote as its own. In most cases, the carvings available seem to be copies of the familiar Spanish figures, essentially caricatures. The Ecuadorian one shown (Fig. 53), however, differs from the Spanish, although it is still readily recognizable.

In sharp contrast to all these figures are the rough-hewn carvings of gauchos from the Argentine (Figs. 54 and 55). They are strong and rather fierce in aspect and obviously the work of skilled carvers. Poses are limited, but details of dress and accoutrements vary widely from piece to piece, indicating that they were individually made with only a basic pattern in mind. They are in a medium-weight wood and stained black all over, as if they were aged oak.

Some idea of what is available elsewhere is illustrated by the three cowboys, each from a different country. The Chilean huaso (Fig. 54) is a modern primitive, while the Peruvian one (Fig. 56) is a once-painted 150-year-old antique, but both are stiff and unnatural. The Brazilian cowboy on a horse isn't even wood, but a copy cast in rubber (Fig. 57)—the result of an all-day search for an example of figure carving in São Paulo by a friend who lives there.

Most of these figures were obviously done with chisel rather than the knife. The tendency in South America, as it is in Europe, is to use a skew chisel or firmer as a knife for carving detail. It has always seemed absurd to me when I see a European-trained carver gripping a chisel near the cutting edge with his finger tips to make it serve as a knife. To me, that kind of job can best be done with a knife, but carvers all over the world have a tendency to make do with the tools they have. Only in traditional European shops making traditional carvings do the carvers have an elaborate set of tools. In the rest of the world, many of the tools are home-made.

CHAPTER IX

Naive Art in Yugoslavia

FOLK OR PRIMITIVE ART occurs in all cultures and usually originates in rural areas. It is spontaneous, simple and unpretentious—most of the artists are self-taught and they draw ideas from their experience, their environment, their imagination. They treat their subjects, usually man and his environment, innocently and simply. Yet, on occasion, such works can be highly fanciful. Some of the work is done to decorate utilitarian objects, but most expresses religious feelings or simply the thoughts of the artist.

Unfortunately, the development of our industrial civilization has brought about a decline and debasement of primitive art. Rural artists migrated to cities to find more lucrative employment, or they became self-conscious of their spare-time carving. Others mass-produced what could be sold, suppressing their own creativity, and even adopting the ideas of other cultures. Thus we find Filipino carvers producing "native" art for Taiwan and Hawaii as well as their own, and the reverse—factories in Seattle producing carvings for Alaskan Eskimos to sell as *their* own. True folk art tends to weaken and die, as it has among the Maori, Balinese, Africans, and over most of Europe. (Interestingly, there is a revival of folk art in the United States—principally as a hobby.)

Most countries have belatedly recognized the value and uniqueness of their folk art and are now making frantic efforts to collect and preserve extant examples. The criterion is not whether the art is *good*, but whether it is *antique* (meaning, in the United States, over 100 years old). In some countries, efforts have been made to revive folk art through local groups, expositions, competitions, and state-sponsored schools or support, but many of these efforts are self-defeating; they tend to encourage the profit-minded rather than the inspired. Also, any training or exposure to others is likely to lead the individual away from primitivism—so folk art dies.

This has been particularly noticeable in Europe and New Zealand, where the state-run schools can no longer find apprentices. It is also beginning in the Far East and the Near East and Africa—industry provides quick money

Figs. 58-60. "Butcher" (left) is a distorted piece that retains the shape of the log from which it was carved by Krešimir Trumbetaš. It is 28½ in (71 cm) tall. "The Rain" (center), by Martin Hegedušić, is 15¾ in (38 cm) tall. The shawl is fine-textured to suggest raindrops; the skirt is vertically grooved. "Widows," by Petar Smajić, suggests a stark existence for both mother and children. It is 19 in (47.5 cm) tall and was carved from a plank.

Note veiner texturing: short & straight for body hair, random arcs for fur coat

Hands & feet crude & large body stubby.

Shallow transverse fluting

Fig. 61. "Prehistoric Man Digging," by Mijo Kuzman, makes effective use of veiner texturing.

Note stubby figure, oversize hands

Oval base like original tree

Base is oval like original tree

Figs. 62 and 63. "Woman Washing" (left), by Dragica Belković, is a 24½-in (61-cm) stump figure with direct and simple outlines. Mato Generalić's "Newlyweds" has distorted proportions to reflect the naiveté of its rural subjects. Note the contrast in hand sizes and the oversized flower.

for less skill and effort. Thus it is rather surprising that a low-key effort to encourage folk art in Yugoslavia has been going on since the 1930s, originally among the artists themselves, and now with some museum and state support. This encouragement has resulted in a considerable body of work, of which some of the best are shown here. They were included in an extensive exhibit which toured the United States in 1977 under the sponsorship of the Smithsonian Institution Traveling Exhibition Service (SITES), which is also the source of all of the photographs reproduced here. The exhibit, incidentally, introduced another word for folk or primitive art—"naive," which like "tribal" may be more descriptive and less deprecating.

These pieces are not slavish copies of earlier masters, but typical of their own environment, distinctive and strong. They are often simple and obvious, and have some general characteristics—stump figures with oversize heads and feet, somewhat brutal features, a lack of decoration or elaboration. There is almost no "embroidery" in the Balinese, Maori, or Japanese manner. Even ordinary texturing of surfaces is relatively rare and is used only to enhance the basic idea, as in the primitive man (Fig. 61) or the woman in the rain (Fig. 59). Many of the pieces follow the outlines of the original wood, so proportions may be sacrificed. The result is a bold, powerful and readily understandable art—something that sophistication and training often kill. The preoccupation is with subject and idea, not with flow and finish. Thus these are excellent and unusual subjects for the neophyte *American* carver. They are, in the original, large enough to require chisels and mallet, and basic shape is more important than detail.

CHAPTER X

Flowing Figures from Bali

ALTHOUGH MOST WHITTLERS and woodcarvers make caricatures, very few distort the human figure to create a design. But the carvers of Bali have always been skilled in working the human body into a flowing design by lengthening or fattening the torso and/or twisting it into a sinuous pose that would be quite impossible to achieve in real life. The results are graceful and interesting carvings well worth emulating.

Most of the present-day carving in Bali is done for the tourist trade because of the chronically poor economy of the island. If a piece sells well, the carver reproduces it in quantity. However, older works were much more individualized, as some of the examples here show. The more unusual ones date from World War II and illustrate the extreme detail and intricacy which is still typical, plus considerable surface decoration and occasional painting of the softer woods. (Most modern figures are in hard woods and unpainted, the surface finish being smooth and reinforced with Kiwi shoe polish.)

Balinese subjects have typically tended to be people, foliage and birds, rather than animals, with religious overtones, because most of the population are pious Hindus given to the worship of Siva. Balinese ancestry is a mix of Indian and Javanese, so both of these influences affect their art, and their carving of wood is more intricate than that done in India, more flowing and less formal or repetitive. Further, their figures are not simply portraits, but are more like candid photographs, as if they were catching their subjects in the course of day-to-day activities.

The flute player, the head hunters and the girl with a flower (Figs. 65, 66 and 70), are the best examples of the human body attenuated into a design. The dancer (Fig. 67) is more typical, although it is also attenuated, and very delicate, particularly compared with the musician and the musing girl (Figs. 64 and 68), which are quite blocky in design.

One of the problems of creating a design with the figure is that it must be supported in position or it will be too fragile. (I know one American bird-carver who is forever repairing his egrets, cranes and shore birds because he

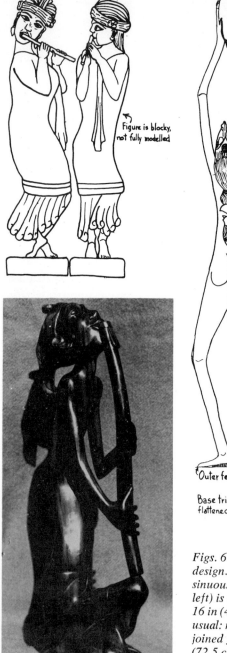

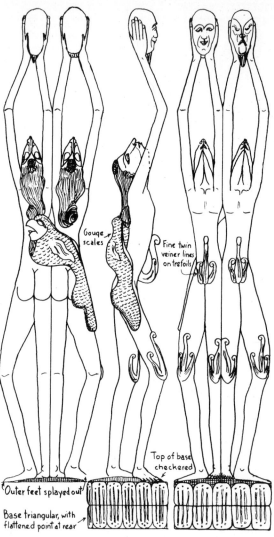

Figure is blocky,
not fully modelled

Gouge
scales

Fine twin
veiner lines
on trefoils

Top of base
checkered

"Outer feet splayed out"

Base triangular, with
flattened point at rear

Figs. 64-66. Two flute players contrast sharply in design. The one above left is "blocky" for a female, sinuous but fairly heavy; the male musician (lower left) is more attenuated and detailed. Both are about 16 in (40 cm) tall. "Headhunter Dance" is quite unusual: rarely are two figures combined, and these are joined from heel to elbow. The assembly is 29 in (72.5 cm) high, and in sawa wood.

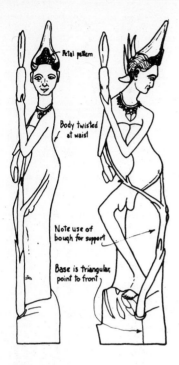

Aerial pattern

Body twisted
at waist

Note use of
bough for support

Base is triangular,
point to front

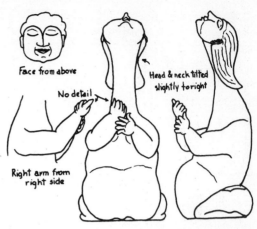

Face from above

No detail

Right arm from
right side

Head & neck tilted
slightly to right

Figs. 67-70. "Dancer" (above left) is a typical attenuated figure emphasizing vertical lines. The musing girl (above) is deliberately distorted and was carved by Bali's top carver, Ida Bagus Tilem. The old farmer (below right) is a 4-ft (1.2-m) piece and dates back about 40 years. The "Girl with Flower" is in ebony and stands 18 in (45 cm) high. See page 78 for photos.

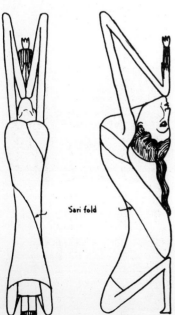

Sari fold

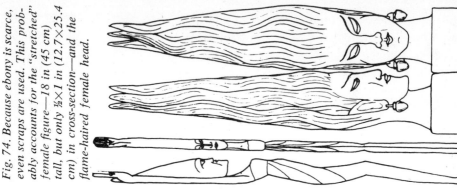

Fig. 74. Because ebony is scarce, even scraps are used. This probably accounts for the "stretched" female figure—18 in (45 cm) tall, but only ¾×1 in (12.7×25.4 cm) in cross-section—and the flame-haired female head.

Basket & cloth Textured by gouge

Overskirt gouge textured

Original 6¼×32"

Fig. 73. Haitian market woman, shown for style contrast, is less graceful and has a scallop texturing around the hips that is repeated in the basket.

Fig. 72. Market woman of Bali is very graceful and has a flower-pattern texturing around the hips.

Fig. 71. Girl in feast costume is of ebony and wears a flower headdress. Note natural foot positions.

insists upon verisimilitude, so the heavy body is carried on extremely fragile legs.) Note that the girl with a flower has the long, thin arms supported by the chin and the dancer has arms and posterior supported by a somewhat artificial trimmed bush.

The willingness to distort a figure to achieve a design is shown quite dramatically by the attenuated female figure and the head with hair rising like flame shown with it in Fig. 74. (By making the face masculine and adding a beard, the latter can be made even taller. The Balinese make a sea god thus, with pebbled surface on upper lip and sideburns.) These suggest a similar treatment of American figures for the carver bold enough to try them; the "attenuated figure" can be made from scrap and is certainly not difficult, and the hair shape is not too difficult either because the long lines flow with the grain of the wood.

Bali and Haiti are interesting to compare because some of their carved figures almost look alike. Carvers of both countries do unusually well with the statuesque female or the wrinkled old man, but the Haitian figures seem to encourage a smile, while the Balinese figures are sober, almost sedate. Compare the Balinese figures of the girl in festive costume and the girl coming from market (Figs. 71 and 72) with the Haitian market woman (Fig. 73), for example, or the old farmer here (Fig. 69) with the resting itinerant from Haiti (Fig. 45). The Balinese emaciated male figure is particularly well done and suggests a willingness to spend time, which is rare in the Western world. The detail of the anatomy is also rather surprising from carvers who have had no formal art training; their understanding of musculature comes almost entirely from observation. The Balinese carver tends to use small tools and many light cuts; this is the secret of the delicate detail which he obtains. The wood is not whacked away initially, leaving it free of rough spots and incipient cracks and splits. Also, he supports the work on his knees or on a soft surface like the ground or a padded platform, so it does not absorb shocks from heavy tools and rigid clamping. Unfortunately, Westerners have never learned to squat like the Orientals and Eastern tailors, so their knees do not form as adequate a cradle. Also, worship of time and knowledge of glues and repairs is greater, so we can afford to risk damaging a carving, confident that we can repair it later.

These figures almost demand a hard, dense-grained wood, so they are not for the knife wielder or the basswood devotee. And they require an amount of time that makes them more suited to the amateur than to the professional, assuming equivalent skill.

The Balinese are also accomplished carvers of the human nude and the pierce-carved panel. They rarely, however, attempt a scenic panel, as the Haitians do. Haitian work, in general, is not as fine as Balinese, and includes many caricatures (probably for the tourist trade), but the two islands, on opposite sides of the world, make strangely similar flowing designs of the human figure.

The secret of carving figures like these is to begin at the top, roughing perhaps half the length, then shaping with small tools and many cuts, leaving details and prominent arms or similar frail elements supported or thick as long as possible. Don't cut at a great distance from the point of support. It is possible to lessen work by sawing the silhouette, but this must be done with care to avoid creating a slender section near the base. It may be helpful to support the piece, particularly in later stages, on a leather or chamois pillow filled with sand, so that the support can conform to the shape of the piece. During early stages, most pieces can be clamped in a vise, the clamp being moved down the piece as the work progresses. Most Balinese pieces are in Macassar ebony imported from the Celebes; this wood is dense enough to support the detail. It goes without saying that your duplicate should be in a similar wood: walnut, teak, cocobola, or ebony itself.

Figs. 75 and 76. "Dancer" (left) and "Girl with Flower." See page 75 for sketches.

CHAPTER XI

Base or No Base—Which?

WHETHER OR NOT a carving should have a base is superficially a matter of taste or circumstance. The human figure, like most mobile devices, tends to terminate in rather unstable bottom surfaces; if it is to stand firmly, it requires a base. Also, we have been trained to expect a base for any three-dimensional figure, just as we expect a frame for any picture. Thus the abstract sculptor finds a piece of beautiful and exotic wood upon which to mount his most recent glob, and the modern puts a pin in a block to support his assemblage of scrap iron.

To the whittler a base can be a problem, because it requires him to bore holes to separate the legs and to chew away wood across grain in order to create a surface which he must then texture in one way or another. The base will give his standing figure stability, but it often also detracts because of its size or rigid shape. On the other hand, a base provides the woodcarver with a means of holding the piece during carving. It offers him a choice between carver's screw and vise, and gives him the freedom to suggest rough or smooth ground, rocks, sea, or however he ultimately textures it. Of 50 small figures of people on my plate rail, 42 have bases.

From the owner's standpoint, the base makes life much simpler. It suggests the amount of space that must be allotted to the carving, gives evidence of one-piece construction in the cases where that is of importance, reduces the likelihood of injury to a leg, contrasts with the supporting surface, even gives a convenient place for a label and/or the carver's signature. But a massive base may check and split the carving, which of itself would adjust to humidity changes.

I have mixed emotions about bases, as the foregoing remarks may indicate. On good carvings—meaning that they take some time, effort and skill—I tend to include a base, but it may or may not be of the same wood as the original. Thus, for example, the squash player has a separate base and the self-made man grows out of one (*see* Chapters 17 and 18).

A base can, and should, be considered as either a help or a hindrance, depending upon the carving. If contact between figure and base is minimal, as in the squash player, an integral base is a constant nuisance during carving, but is essential for display, so it can be added later. For some figures, a base of contrasting or exotic wood can enhance the value of the carving. A rosewood base, for example, suggests that what's above is worthwhile. In a figure, the grain normally should be vertical and adding a horizontal-grained base may provide a pleasing contrast. But, in general, the thick, squared-off base for a light and lithe figure is anathema; the base should also be light and thin, or very tall, not just a block. If it is integral and massive, it should be hollowed out somewhat underneath to inhibit checking and rocking.

Balinese carvers show more imagination in the matter of bases than do most others. They often use a triangle, perhaps because they split wood in triangles from relatively small-diameter trees. (That makes as much sense as our using a rectangular base because the blank was a plank.) But a triangle provides one corner for each foot and a third for the base of a net, or a background stump, or a larger area to support the buttocks of a seated figure and a narrow one for extended feet. I don't advocate a triangle necessarily, but it is at least something different. An oval or a circle or a free-form shape can be as effective. I merely suggest that the base can contribute rather than confine.

The sides of the base can help as well, if properly treated. They can suggest the terrain or carry a simple design—anything to avoid a flat and uninteresting block, unless the carving is of itself so interesting that the block will not be noticed.

Lastly, there is the matter of base size. The conventional base is the size of the original block. That is faulty. If there is a base, it should look like it can and does support the figure, but not be so obtrusive that the figure dare not move off it. A larger base may give more solidity and save wood and time if added later; but often a figure is more dramatic if an elbow or foot projects over the base (increasing the risk of damage when displayed).

CHAPTER XII

How About Surface Texture?

WOODCARVERS are given to repeating the old, old saying that many carvings are ruined in the finishing. That is true, of course, because many carvers use whatever finish they have available or have used before, and their taste may be regrettably bad. Cheap carvings, particularly from underdeveloped countries, were frequently doused with shellac or cheap varnish, and some American carvings were (and are) finished the same way, making them shine like cheap furniture. This has encouraged purists to use no finish whatsoever, or simply oil and wax, although this combination is at times unsuitable as well, depending upon wood, exposure, humidity and occasional other factors, including insect infestation.

Some primitive carvers have felt their way into much more specialized finishes of many kinds, ranging from natural dyes to a "secret" formula used by a few carvers in Haiti and which gives a head or bust a smooth but slightly dusty surface exactly matching the complexion of some native women. What many of these carvers are actually striving for is not a finish, but a *texture* that somehow simulates or suggests the natural.

Quality wood sculptures commonly have one of two surface textures, either smooth and polished, which emphasizes the figure, color and grain of the wood; or tool marks, planes or surface patterns to emphasize the carving or the figure itself. The low-gloss finish is by far the most common, perhaps because the sculptor is more adept with sandpaper and riffler files than with sharp-edged tools, or because the wood proves recalcitrant. The textured surface may also be added after the carving, simply as an allover pattern of small scallops that catch the light without having any relationship to the strokes actually used in cutting and shaping.

Occasionally, artists break these patterns and strive for a surface that will have a dramatic look or feel or create a particular response of the figure to light, just as artists in other media apply pigments with a palette knife or leave the tool marks or fingermarks showing on a clay model. Some carvers actually develop a surface finish that eventually becomes a sort of personal

Figs. 77 and 78. Stylized "Mother and Child" (left) is in mahogany and about 12 in (30 cm) high. It was sandpapered smooth, and antiqued. "Old Man of the Sea" was carved in a greyed piece of driftwood. Hair and beard were textured with V-grooves blunted at the bottom to resemble fluter cuts.

trademark and others simply drift into coloring their work out of simple frustration.

These figures from Mexico, Bali, New Guinea and Haiti illustrate the point. "Mars," in carving the Haitian mother and child (Fig. 77), relied upon the silhouette for strength and design, so finished his piece smooth, with many of the lines fading into the body of the piece. He did not detail the features, the digits, or the musculature. He was striving for a smooth, flowing, harmonious shape, the result being reminiscent of many Balinese carvings.

In contrast, "Maurice" amplified the erosion of a piece of driftwood into a pattern of fillets which simultaneously produces the effect of hair and frames the face (Fig. 78). More than half the area is thus textured, so light tends to bring out the smooth surface of the face within a greyed or softer aureole of hair and beard. Pigments have been rubbed in to add a bit of color to lips, cheeks, teeth and eyes, but their effect is only to tint the grey wood slightly.

The two Mexican Virgins of Soledad (Figs. 79 and 80) are much more primitive than the preceding two figures. They have obviously been copied from earlier models, but have been stylized and interpreted as well. Crown, face, hands and flower are modelled, but the rest of the figure is primarily silhouette. The robe surface, however, is textured to suggest the opulent embroidery of the cloth robe. In one example, the irregular pattern is painstakingly produced with stamps—one a ⅜-in (9.6-mm) circle and the others a ⅜- and ⅛-in (9.6-and 3.2-mm) straight line. The wood, like pine, is soft and preserves the stamp pattern clearly. The figure, overall, is only 8½ in (21.6 cm) high. In the other figure, the pattern is incised.

Figs. 79 and 80. Two versions of the Virgin of Soledad (Mexico) are alike in the overall patterns in robe and skirt, although the one at left was textured with punches, the other with knife cuts.

The two dancers, carved in Mexico City a score of years before I acquired them, represent two of the traditional tribal dances of Mexico: one is the deer dance of Sonora (Fig. 81), the other the feather or plume dance of Oaxaca (Fig. 82). Both dancers are in animated poses, and the carver has contributed to their animation by giving them slightly blurred outlines and avoiding sharp detail, and, as a result, they appear to be caught in motion, particularly the plume dancer. The figures were rather carefully shaped, then the majority of each surface was textured—the deer dancer with parallel channeling by a small gouge, the plume dancer with scallops produced by a larger, flatter gouge. Neither face is detailed, although that of the deer dancer has a nose shape and a fortuitous placement of channels to suggest the mouth and eyes, both on the dancer and on the deer. Texturing covers most of the body surfaces of the dancers, except for the feet (which are presumably solidly supporting the figure), and a few other details. In the deer dancer, these are the ears and horns of the deer head (this is an assumption on my part because I had to replace missing parts) and the gourd rattles (maracas) in the hands. The gouge lines are not all parallel, but in some cases suggest lines of movement or of stress, as across the shoulders and the chest.

The plume dancer wears the familiar headdress, cape and apron, with the apron practically blended into the lines of the body. The cape, however, in real life ornately embroidered, is smoothed and patterned with stain. The headdress is regularly patterned with larger gouge scallops to suggest rows of feathers, but has an essentially smooth surface, while that of the real-life headdress is much rougher.

This particular carver, by the way, used a finishing technique that preserved, but partially obliterated, the lines of his carving. He apparently poured melted beeswax over the entire surface, so that it congealed and collected in all the hollows. Over the years, this clouded and collected dust, so it was necessary to scrape off larger accumulations, then alternately heat and wipe to get rid of most of it. No solvent available would dissolve this hard wax—as chemists who use hydrofluoric acid know, because they store it in wax bottles.

There are a number of other examples of surface texturing in other chapters. Each is mentioned as it occurs—like lining for hair, cross-hatching for roughness, and so on. They are worthy of a little thought and may give your work more real "polish" than can gloss varnish.

The pregnant woman from Iriana, New Guinea (Fig. 83), is somewhat Balinese in style and pose, particularly the head and hair, but differs sharply

Fig. 81. This "Deer Dancer" was surface-textured with gouge lines over a blocky silhouette. Texturing changes angle in stress areas. The only untextured areas are the antlers, rattles, and feet. The piece is 16 in (40 cm) tall.

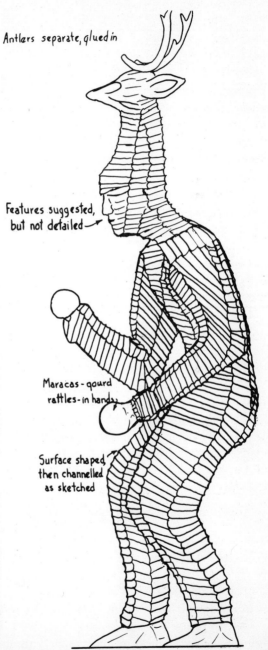

Antlers separate, glued in

Features suggested, but not detailed →

Maracas - gourd rattles - in hands

Surface shaped, then channelled as sketched

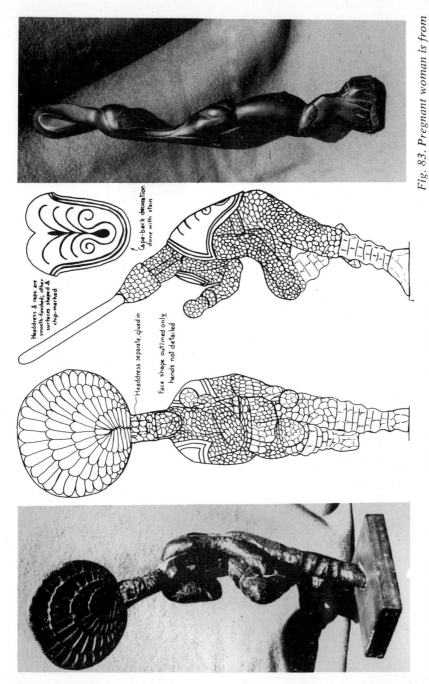

Fig. 83. Pregnant woman is from New Guinea and surprisingly sophisticated. It was finished smooth and stained black for a low-gloss effect.

Headdress & cape are smooth-finished; other surfaces shaped & chip-marked

Cape-back decoration done with stain

Headdress separate, glued in

Face shape outlined only; hands not detailed

Fig. 82. "Feather Dancer" was carved by the same artist as Fig. 81, and in mahogany. Face and hands are not detailed, and all but the cape and feet are covered with small scallops.

in its arms, one of which is almost twice as long as the other. Also, the hands and feet are misproportioned, and the leg as short as the arm. The carver has accentuated the smooth curves of the figure by giving it a smooth, low-gloss surface as well. The base wood is light in color, so the figure was stained black, then rubbed lightly with grey or white pigment to give a dark-grey color. The only detailing of this primitive figure (which is surprisingly sophisticated in general design and treatment) is the veiner shading around the loincloth; otherwise tool marks and sharp edges have been removed. By contrast, a male figure from the same general area is primitive and blocky, with long gouge and firmer lines left in, as if the figure had been roughed out and then abandoned.

There are many other aspects of texturing, of course, including effects obtained by utilizing the figure or grain of the wood itself. In most cases, the carver positions his work, or modifies his design, to take advantage of surface irregularities or imperfections, like knots or color changes, or selects the piece of wood because its shape suggests the ultimate carving. In other cases, the carver must adapt his design to the shape of the available wood, so he makes a virtue of necessity.

The Japanese have long used the grain in still another way. They carve turtles, badgers, frogs, toads, goldfish and dragons in a cedar that has alternating hard (dark) and soft (lighter) stripes in the grain, and then erode the soft wood so that the surface has a series of ridges. The same technique has been used in this country on pine, redwood and cypress to create the effect of aging (we have done it by sandblasting), and has recently been "discovered" by tyro carvers. Another texturing technique is pyrography, used commonly by bird carvers to simulate the veining of feathers. A pyrographic needle can make the equivalent of veiner cuts with a dark-brown surface burned on, and can be quite dramatic in suggesting feathers, fur or long hair on light-colored wood figures.

CHAPTER XIII

Composites and Assemblies

MANY CARVED FIGURES, particularly large ones, are not single pieces, but composites of a number of pieces assembled by gluing, or with articulated joints, and many are made of more than one material, for one reason or another. Sometimes the composite is made because wood of the required shape and size is not available; because there is danger of checking or warping; because weight must be held down; because the pose develops problems with grain or wastes inordinate amounts of material; because the subject requires a material other than wood be incorporated to achieve a particular effect; because the figure must be posed; or simply because the carver expects to save time and effort by assembling components. In production operations, composites may make it possible for some components to be produced largely by machine or by less-skilled workers, leaving only the specialized work for the master carver. Sculptors have worked this way for centuries.

I have shown dozens of composite figures in this and previous books, some of them articulated toys, some rigid religious figures. The four shown here, however, are composite figures designed for a particular purpose. Although the Finnish man (Fig. 84) has head and hands as finely carved as any I have seen, the carver contented himself with those and the boots, while the body and clothes are of cloth. He demonstrated his skill in fine features (the lips have a slight curve at the left to accommodate a dangling cigarette) and detailed hands, but he was essentially producing a costume doll rather than a carving, and the cloth elements of the body provide the necessary flexibility for dressing and posing. Also, the body is covered anyway. . . . The right hand, however, is perfectly carved and tinted, even though it is thrust into a pocket.

This figure, probably the product of a family enterprise, is like a great many dolls of past centuries, which had wood or china heads and appendages, but bodies of cloth or leather, more or less realistically stuffed. With seams at joints, the figure was flexible enough to pose in a variety of positions.

The German doll (Fig. 86), drawn full scale, is a composite made almost entirely of wood. Her arms and legs are abnormally long and thin and she has no knee joints, but her arms and legs move quite realistically and her thin arms and legs make dress design and application easier. Only the head and appendages were enamelled in color. I replaced an arm and a leg for the doll, which is displayed in a local historical museum, and liked the design so well that I made my own of maple, using dowels for the arms and legs and modifying the connections inside to utilize modern screw eyes and wire links as sketched.

The form of the hip and elbow joints is, incidentally, the same as that used on a Chamula man and woman (Fig. 85), carved on the other side of the world, although the latter have fully carved bodies with integral legs and head, and articulation only in the elbows. Because the Chamulas are modern, the Indians used brads or short lengths of wire for the axles instead of the traditional thin wooden ones. There is less friction with them and they're stronger, if you're not a sentimentalist.

Fig. 84. This Finnish figure, 10 in (25 cm) high, has carefully detailed head, hands, and boots. The body is sewn cloth, topped by tailored clothes, and the hat can (and does) come off.

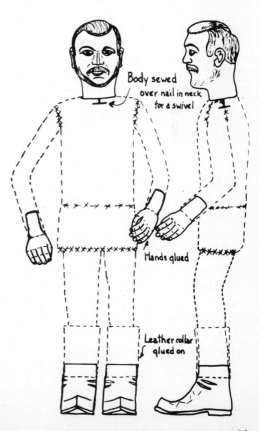

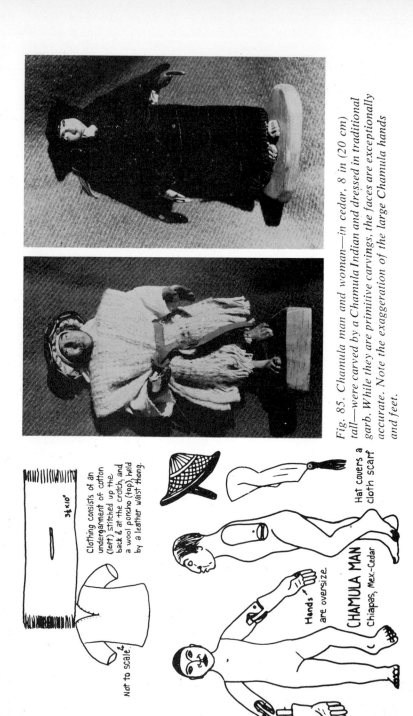

Fig. 85. Chamula man and woman—in cedar, 8 in (20 cm) tall—were carved by a Chamula Indian and dressed in traditional garb. While they are primitive carvings, the faces are exceptionally accurate. Note the exaggeration of the large Chamula hands and feet.

Clothing consists of an undergarment of cotton (left) stitched up the back & at the crotch, and a wool poncho (top), held by a leather waist thong.

3½ × 10"

Not to scale.

Hat covers a cloth scarf

Hands are oversize

CHAMULA MAN
Chiapas, Mex.—Cedar

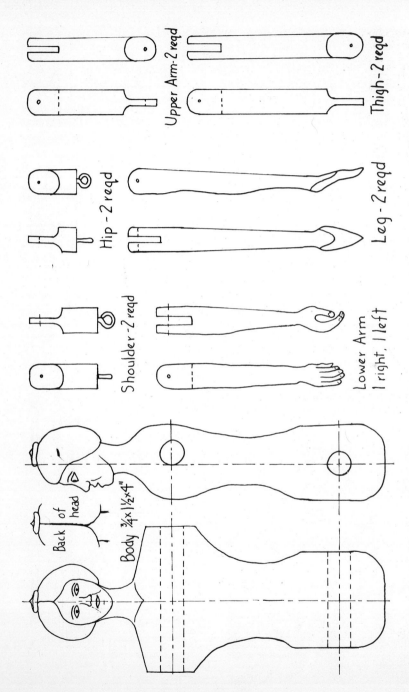

Upper Arm - 2 reqd

Thigh - 2 reqd

Hip - 2 reqd

Leg - 2 reqd

Shoulder - 2 reqd

Lower Arm
1 right, 1 left

Back of head

Body ¾ × 1½ × 4"

Fig. 86. This 19th-century stick doll is from Germany and was probably made thin of limb to facilitate dressing. Arms and legs were carved from dowels; the body and head are one piece. See photo on page 92.

The Chamula are, incidentally, a large tribe of Mayan derivation, living in and around San Cristóbal de las Casas, high in the mountains of southern Mexico. They have the Mayan nose, tend to be dark-skinned, are short and stocky, with relatively large hands and feet. The two figures from there are accurate averages, but the carver used female torsos for both, a fact hidden by the clothing. This, by the way, is how the Chamulas dressed 20 years ago and some still do today, though many have adopted jeans, dresses, and typical mestizo clothing, at least for town. The figures are in cedar, and represent some of the most accurate primitive carving I've seen. The uplifted foot on the man helps to avoid rigidity in the pose. Despite the accuracy of the faces, the figures are caricatures because the hands and feet have been overemphasized, thus making the forearms too short.

I still remember, after 40 years, a group of life-size statues of saints carved for a Catholic church in New Jersey. Because the parishioners were Negroes, the statues were negroid, the heads, arms and exposed body portions being of walnut, while the robes were in stainless steel. These figures were extremely dramatic composites, done with great skill and taste. It is also possible to combine various colors of wood in producing human figures, somewhat like three-dimensional marquetry, even to make low- or medium-relief plaques in this fashion, by assembling various colors and grains of wood in body-element-shaped blocks rather than in rectangular ones. The effect is closely akin to a jigsaw puzzle in assembly, and permits of no variation in outlines, but can be very dramatic.

Fig. 87. Nineteenth-century composite doll from Germany.

CHAPTER XIV

High Relief Permits Realistic Scenes

HIGH-RELIEF CARVING was, until perhaps 100 years ago, quite commonly done in Europe and Japan, and, by extension, in the United States. It was the common form of carved decoration in palaces and mansions, churches, temples and monasteries. Panels were incorporated in heavy furniture, such as chests and cabinets, applied in over-mantels, door frames and ceilings, even on walls. Much of the private decoration was composed of bucolic scenes involving people and animals with a background of trees and shrubbery, but in churches and monasteries it covered a wide range of religious subjects, from depictions of saints to the Stations of the Cross.

High-relief carvings usually incorporate a number of figures, often carved in the round, to depict a scene against a foreshortened background that serves as the equivalent of a stage setting (and which may include medium and/or low relief, as many museum dioramas do). Forced perspective is commonly employed. The most famous English carver, Grinling Gibbons, who commonly carved swags of flowers and fruit, was, in fact, criticized (and still is) for occasionally carving his subject in the round and appliquéing it to a panel. This permitted him to work from both back and front, and lessened the problem of how much undercutting was necessary—a problem which still plagues anyone who undertakes a high-relief carving. His favorite material was limewood, although he also worked in other woods, bronze and stone, and his work has never been surpassed in Europe. Some of his swags, in St. Paul's, London, and other English buildings, tremble at the slightest vibration—and have been trembling for almost 300 years.

The vulnerability of high-relief carving (both during and after carving) may be one of the factors that led to its decline. Others are: changing tastes in decoration, reduced availability of thick wood, and greater consciousness of time. In high-relief carving, a relatively enormous amount of wood must be cut away, unless frontal figures are appliquéd. Also, the completed work is fragile, a real dust-catcher, and has a tendency to appear florid and overdone by modern standards. Thus, high relief is relatively rare in the modern world, perhaps unjustifiably so. It is quite easy to do, compared with medium or low relief, because the third dimension is more nearly correct. It offers a considerable challenge to the carver equipped with the necessary tools, time and skill, and is an interesting variation to the usual flat panels in which the third dimension must be subordinated, if not almost lost.

I am providing here four examples of high-relief carving, one an antique and the other three quite modern. It is interesting that the modern examples come from Spain, which is one of the few countries outside the United States where some high-relief carving of panels is still done. The older example is a panel carved in Austria after an 1869 painting by Franz DeFregger (1835-1921). Ken Evans, of Portland, Oregon, owns the unsigned carving (Fig. 88) and has made extensive inquiries about it. It is probably a copy of the painting, but the painter was originally a carver who didn't study painting until he was 25 years old, and the painting was made nine years later in Munich. (The painting is in the Tiroler Landesmuseum Ferdinandeum in Innsbruck, Austria.) Did DeFregger make the carving, then copy it later in oils, or did some unknown make the carving? Nobody knows, which is at least a minor argument in favor of signing carvings—something that European carver-craftsmen did not do often, because their work was often copied from paintings.

The subject of both painting and carving comes from an actual occurrence in 1809. Josef Speckbacher, the central figure, was a leader under the Tyrolean patriot, Andreas Hoffer. He was meeting with others at an inn when some of his men discovered that his eight-year-old son, Anderl, was actively participating in the fight for Tyrolean freedom against the French and Bavarians, obviously without the advice or consent of his father. In the picture, a Schutze (marksman) of the Freedom Fighters is returning the son to his father (Fig. 89). Note, in the carving, the almost free-standing figures, the complexity of the wall decorations, the detail in the "wall painting" of the Madonna and Child (Fig. 90) and the fully carved little wagon at upper right. Which was first, painting or carving? And who carved the panel? The carving is 4 × 24 × 20 in (10 × 61 × 51 cm), and weighs 37 lbs (16.6 kg) with its wide and elaborate frame (not shown). The wood is cembra pine. The carver shows textures on the deer horn and wrinkles on the faces, as well as defining hair and other details.

This is an excellent example of the use of high relief to tell a story, rather than being limited to the depiction of an individual or group, as a three-dimensional single figure normally is. It shows a familiar subject, and the

Figs. 88-90. The above carving is 4 in (10 cm) thick, roughly 20×24 in (50×60 cm), and includes every detail of the painting from which it was taken. Close-up (below right) of marksman and boy shows how the illusion of depth was obtained. Note the free-standing figures and perspective size-reduction. Other close-up shows detail of antlers and the low-relief miniature of the Madonna and Child.

Fig. 91. "Final Chapter," a 2 x 9 x 23½-in (5 x 22 x 35-cm) panel from Córdoba, Spain, depicts Cervantes writing at a desk, and the image of a dying Don Quixote and a grieving Sancho Panza above his head. Depth of the carving is 1½ in (38 mm) in deepest areas.

Cervantes profile

Spain Chestnut(?)

Panza profile

Arm & bod of Quixote

Back rounded to thin panel ends

Quixote profile

at end of beard

at end of rt. hand

Head of Cervantes

carver was therefore able to base his work on fact—even if his "fact" is only a painting—and he wasn't forced to stylize because his knowledge did not extend to precise details.

As mentioned earlier, Spain is obsessed with the story of Don Quixote, and the story is quite familiar to the tourist world, so it is natural that many carvings depict at least the principal figures in the story. Thus, available three-dimensional figures in that country show Don Quixote and Sancho Panza in an endless variety of poses, afoot or on horseback. However, in Córdoba, I found a number of panels depicting scenes in the story, usually having to do with the battle with the windmill and Quixote's resulting discomfiture, but the one illustrated here (Fig. 91) was exceptional. It depicts Cervantes writing the last chapter of the book (or so I interpret it), the scene above showing Don Quixote dying with the ever-faithful Panza looking very concerned. It is thus a scene within a scene, perhaps similar to a cartoonist's drawing of a balloon depicting a thought over the head of the thinker. In any case, it provides a picture that no single 3-D figure could, and, from the constructional standpoint, includes faces in profile, full view and at an angle. What's more, in each case the face is expressing a particular emotion—and none is the stock caricature grin. The profiled face is by far the easiest pose to carve, regardless of depth of relief. Full face is somewhat more complicated because of the projecting nose and subtler differences in facial planes. Part-view or angle faces offer problems because curves must be modified; in this sculpture, even the professional had some problems with Panza's face.

The Moneylender panel represents a somewhat more conventional treatment of high relief (Figs. 92 and 93). It was produced as one of a series of subjects by the best-known of the Spanish carving factories, Ouro. It is actually a combination of various relief thicknesses, the central figure and the bookshelves being in low relief, the shelves with the pottery in medium relief—bringing them to the level of the outside "frame," about ½ in (12.7 mm) above the background—and the outer figures in high relief—about 1¼ in (31.7 mm) deep, or ¾ in (19 mm) outside the frame. These various heights can be distinguished in the angular view (Fig. 94).

In carving a panel, there is always the question of framing the subject. The Cervantes panel is allowed simply to "bleed" off the edges. The framing becomes whatever is behind it, and presumably of a contrasting tint or color. (The panel itself is quite dark.) Also, to avoid any feeling of massiveness or thickness, the carver has rounded off the top and bottom from the back, so the effect is one of lightness belying the basic 2-in (5-cm) thickness of the panel itself. Contrast this treatment with the more conventional self-framing of *The Moneylender*, or the partial silhouette of *Tryst* (Fig. 95), a quite modern handling. Most formal of all is the framing of the Austrian panel, which has a heavy and wide carved border to make the carving itself appear as if almost in a shadowbox, an effect accentuated by the forward-sloping floor, which makes it necessary to box the sides and the top of the finished carving to bring it up to framing level.

Thus we have four variations in framing—from nothing to a full box—although in three of the four subjects some part of the carving projects; even in *The Moneylender* panel, the self-frame is only about half the thickness of the two outer figures at their shoulders, as can be seen in the angled photograph (Fig. 94). The house wall provides a convenient background in *Tryst*, but it is broken by the recessed door and window, the projecting eave and the ground level below the suitor's feet. This helps create a feeling of reality from the shadows, regardless of where the panel is hung. On the Cervantes panel, the unframed treatment helps to create the illusion that each of the

Fig. 92. *"The Moneylender" is a carving-factory product from Spain. It is in chestnut, 1¾×9×15½ in (4.5×22×39 cm), with a background that is ½ in (12.7 mm) thick, and an integral frame that is 1 in (25.7 mm) thick. See also Figs. 93 and 94.*

two scenes extends beyond the limits of the panel itself. If it were framed, it would be constricted and its unusual proportion of length to width might be displeasing.

Framing of a panel can be extremely important. A painting is, despite any effort at texturing by the artist, essentially flat, so its frame can enhance the third dimension. In a carving, the frame may constrict and inhibit the effect, as is evident in most old high-relief carvings. It is often much more effective to subordinate or eliminate the conventional frame, so that the carving itself is dominant and unconfined.

High-relief carving, of course, requires a great deal of roughing with gouges, and the dangers of splitting or over-cutting are constant. In most instances, the use of a router will save relatively little time. One way to reduce the time and cost of wood is to appliqué blocks in the areas which project

Figs. 93 and 94. "Thè Moneylender" panel (left): The central figure and bookshelves are in low relief; the pottery shelves are in medium relief. Angled photograph shows the various kinds of relief carving that were combined and reveals how much under-cutting was done.

farthest, even to saw the blocks to the approximate silhouette before they are appliquéd. In work of this sort it is extremely important, of course, to make stop cuts across the grain first and to set in accurately. Templates of the various elements and even a sketch on transparent vellum will help in maintaining location, because guide lines are almost impossible to retain. Most important of all is to have a clear mental picture of the composition, so that you can remember to leave wood for such elements as the deer horns and Madonna picture on the background of the Austrian example, as well as to retain the various levels of the picture. In ivory carving, this problem is reduced by carving the scene in thin panels, then assembling them like a sandwich in a frame. This can also be done with wood, but the larger scale makes the trick evident in most instances.

Fig. 95. "Tryst" is an interesting high-relief composition from Spain. Its dimensions are 2×7¾×11 in (5×20×27.5 cm). Note that mother and daughter were carved in the round, as was the suitor, and all were undercut to make them stand out.

CHAPTER XV

Lower Relief and Modelling

IF HIGH-RELIEF CARVING is accompanied by problems in deciding how much undercutting is necessary, lower-relief carving brings similar problems in modelling.

Most present-day relief carving is quite shallow, with backgrounds sunk as little as ⅛ in (3.2 mm) on small plaques and ½ in (12.7 mm) or 1 in (25.4 mm) on larger ones. The illusion of greater depth is obtained by darkening or texturing the background, by pierce-carving, or by silhouetting the subject so that there is little or no background of the wood itself. This makes modelling and forced perspective extremely important; so important, in fact, that many carvers make mistakes and their panels have a "wooden" look (forgive the pun). Others are extremely intricate, containing so much detail, plus efforts to undercut, that they become fussy and over-detailed, losing their strength in more ways than one.

Figs. 96 and 97. Philippine women, in mahogany and 2 in (5 cm) thick, are almost half-relief. Each has an integral-carved earring. Because of the depth, modelling is relatively easy.

Here I have attempted to combine a great many widely differing subjects and techniques to provide a sort of index of low and medium relief, and of modelling, and to show how and where they differ from in-the-round, which is quite similar to high-relief carving. Consider, for example, the two silhouette panels in mahogany from the Philippines (Figs. 96 and 97), typical of the technique commonly in use there. Each is 10 × 13 in (25.4 × 33 cm), but carved from 2-in (5-cm) wood. This thickness, combined with the silhouetting and modelling, makes the carvings appear almost in-the-round, except for a flat back. The carver actually achieves considerable depth in modelling the face around the eyes and neck, which gives the face a natural look. Further, he carved the earrings free, using the old "chain trick" to achieve an effect.

Similar examples include the two women in Figure 98. The woman with child on the left is from Haiti, and the pregnant woman (with fetus outline pierce-carved in her abdomen) is from Costa Rica, yet they are strangely analogous, both in design and technique. The third dimension in both works is about half of actual size at the shoulders and hips; the effect is a double-sided medium-relief silhouette. Both are rather squared off as to torso; only the heads are modelled in the round, and neither details the face or arms. (For another photo of the Haitian woman, see Fig. 77, p. 82.)

The high modelling of medium relief is also obtained in the woman-and-child panel (Fig. 99) and the bullfighter panel from Ecuador (Fig. 101), as well as in the series of Indians and other figures from the Pátzcuaro area of Mexico (Fig. 102). The Mexican carver, or carvers, was not nearly so skilled in technique, but these figures have a crude strength, nonetheless. The carver let his imagination run free. Some of the full figures are 6 ft tall (1.8 m); all are at least 1 in (25.4 mm) thick, in soft wood. Sharply contrasting in size is the small head of a girl from Ecuador (Fig. 100), with its somewhat stylized face (accented nose and eyebrow outline), which is actually in the round in wood 1 in (25.4 mm) thick, framed by the hair at the top and brought to a pointed and thin tress below to provide delicate, balanced support on the base.

In all of these carvings, modelling is not much of a problem because the third dimension is deep. The difficulties increase as thickness is reduced, so that planes and apparent relative elevations become increasingly important. Familiar handlings of this problem are depicted in the little Indian-head pendant from Peru (Fig. 103) and the copy of an antique candle sconce from Spain (Fig. 105). The Peruvian carver made use of a triangle of wood to get an approximate face silhouette—a technique also used by the Maya and the Celts before we reinvented it in recent years as a way of getting proper face modelling. Because he used the triangle, the face itself is actually low relief. In the case of the candle sconce, the original carver sloped the support back above the eyes, thus achieving a projecting nose in another way. (This figure is primitive, to be sure, but note the strong stylizing and consequent dramatic effect.)

Still lower relief is used in the next series of examples. In the ebony pendant of the Mayan head (Fig. 104), overall thickness is only about ⅛ in (3.2 mm), but I used stylizing to define the headdress, cheek and eye, and accentuated this by inlaying ivory for the eyeball and earring. The Haitian-head pendant has an inserted earring for similar contrast. Ruth Hawkins in Brasstown, North Carolina, contrasted her two angels in holly (Fig. 106) by mounting them on a strongly patterned cross-section of branch, which ties the composition together and silhouettes the figures.

Robert Gurend of Haiti, who carved the vase (Figs. 107 and 108), is a street artist, working largely with two tools, a firmer and a V-tool, with a club serving as a mallet. He starts with rough-turned shapes of soft wood and holds them on his knees, so he can carry his shop in a shopping bag. His work is consistently strong because he understands the importance of having a single center of interest, accented by the carving technique. Thus the base and rim of this vase, as well as the minor collar, are decorated with simple V-tool patterns and the lower bulge with a floral design also done with the V-tool. This simply separates it from the uncarved base itself. The neck of the vase, however, is deeply carved and modelled, albeit primitive and stylized. The woman and the burro are the center of interest and stand out from the background, an effect accentuated by trenching or grooving the background around them. The trees and basket serve merely to fill out the perimeter of the band and can be amplified or reduced as necessary. This, by the way, provides a good example of how to adjust a design to fit a surface, a common problem in relief-carving, of irregular objects. Gurend changes the design on each vase to avoid boredom.

In working out a design on a surface, or in carving shaped objects and plaques, it may be enough to use very little modelling, leaving much of the surface flat and undisturbed. An excellent case in point is a tabletop which, if carved at all, should have minimum-depth surface carving, so the stability of objects placed upon it will not be imperiled. Also, fewer crevices are thereby provided for the accumulation of dust and dirt. (This, of course, is

Figs. 98-101. A surprising coincidence (above): The figure at left is from Haiti, that at right from Costa Rica. Both are two-sided reliefs, and only the heads are in-the-round. Mahogany panel from Ecuador (above right) is 11½ in (29 cm) tall, ¾ in (19 mm) thick. The stylized head from Ecuador (below right) is turned 90°, so hair is both frame and support. Toreador and bull, also from Ecuador, was pierced and silhouetted, and looks deeper than it is.

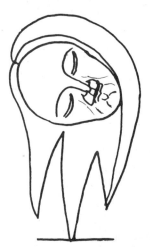

DANCER† CAMPESINO† QUIXOTE†   MARDI GRAS   FARMER

Note: Detail varies
as does design truth

Fig. 102. Sketches of primitive Mexican figures from Pátzcuaro.

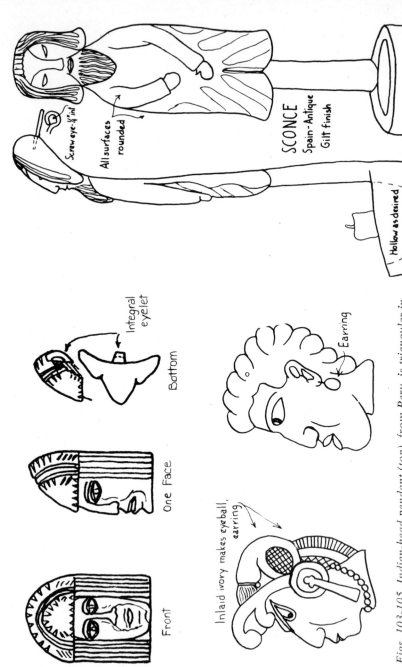

Screw eye ¼' int

All surfaces rounded

SCONCE
Spain - Antique
Gilt finish

Hollow as desired

Integral eyelet

Bottom

Earring

One Face

Front

Inlaid ivory makes eyeball, earring

Figs. 103-105. Indian-head pendant (top). from Peru, is triangular in cross-section. Maya profile, contrasted here with one from Haiti, was carved in ebony. with very low relief. The copy of an antique candle sconce (right) was carved in soft wood. Note the exaggerated nose and brow lines.

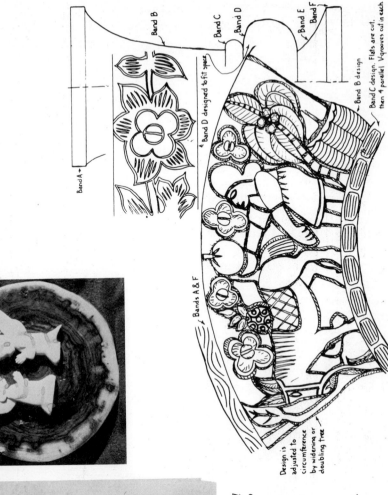

Fig. 106. These angels, carved in low relief in holly, would be lost as silhouettes unless placed against a contrasting background.

Band A →

Band B

Band C

Band D

Band E

Band F

← Band D designed to fit space

← Band B design

← Band C design. Flats are cut, then 4 parallel V-grooves cut in each

← Bands A & F

Design is adjusted to circumference by widening or doubling tree →

Figs. 107 and 108 (above and right). The woman and burro on the neck of this turned softwood vase are the center of interest, so the other surfaces are subordinated. The design is stylized and primitive, but lifted above the background by bosting and grooving around each figure.

107

less important if the carving is to be covered with glass, but some compromise must be arrived at between the amount of wood surface there is to support the glass and its thickness.) The design should be worked out so that any complex or deep carving is away from the areas where stability is needed. A flat tabletop I saw in Bali had large and flat floral designs at the points where service and salad plates, saucers and centerpiece would normally be placed, while the rest of the surface was actually deep-relief and pierce-carved.

It is not always necessary to work over an entire surface and to blend all lines and model all contours; it may, in fact, be better on occasion *not* to do so. One factor is the grain of the wood. If it is strong and lovely of itself, carving should be subordinated or even omitted. Any effort to subdue a strong grain with even stronger carving usually ends in confusion for both carver and viewer. Again, if the wood is old and has a desirable patina, minimal carving will help to preserve the patina. If it is a chair back—or, worse still, a chair seat—minimal carving will be appreciated by any sitter.

In addition to the questions raised in the preceding paragraph, there are those having to do with technique. Should the design have crisp, sharp edges, or should it be modelled? Should it be trenched, leaving the background high around it, self-framed, or have the background bosted away? Should the lowered visual effect of shallow relief carving be compensated for by darkening the background or the lines of the carving itself as a scrimshander does? How much should line width be varied, groove-angle changed? Should surface texturing be used, and if so, should it be with veiner, V-tool or knife? Cross-hatched or gouge-scalloped?

Many of the answers to these questions depend upon personal taste, and I find myself varying from panel to panel, often simply to see what effect I can get. Any modelling or texturing breaks up impinging light and changes the apparent tone of what the observer sees. Thus, gouge-scalloping, cross-hatching or parallel-lining will make a surface appear darker because the reflected light isn't beamed as it is from a flat surface. Textured areas tend to sink back, an effect which can be enhanced by "antiquing" them—going over them with a slightly darker stain and immediately wiping most of it away, except in the deepest areas. (This is actually an "instant patina"— because true patina is merely the accumulation of dirt, grease, dust and such over a long period of time, and it is naturally heavier in the grooves and hollows.)

I find that irregular grooving tends to create the effect of slightly wavy

Figs. 109 and 110. Head of Tarahumara Indian (left), in cedar, was trench-carved and is self-bordered. The study of Benito Juarez is in mahogany and has various V-grooves detailing general features.

hair; regular and precise grooving suggests hair drawn tight to the scalp; fine veiner lines suggest fine hair (except on small figures, when *no* lines suggests even finer hair); and coarser lines suggest a pelt or coarse hair, as in a lion's mane. Tilting a V-tool away from one edge, thus lengthening the other side of the groove, tends to make the sharper side rise visually above the wider one. As the depth of relief is reduced, the effect of even slight variations in surface level and modelling becomes greater, so hollow cheeks and the like can be obtained with very shallow shaping. Also, with very shallow relief, crisp edges will stand out, rounded edges will disappear (an argument against sandpaper also). Trenching does not take away from the carving—see the Indian and Juarez (Figs. 109 and 110). It saves a lot of fussing over background and protects the carving itself. Framing is often confining and more trouble than it is worth.

The answers to others of the preceding questions, and perhaps additional ones, will become apparent by study of the shallow-carved panels. I carved the Tarahumara Indian (Fig. 109) from memory in Mexico, in a piece of cedar, using only a pocketknife. The high-set cheekbones are suggested by

109

Figs. 111 and 112. Two breadboards, in cherry, are 7×11 in (17.5×27.5 cm). The one at left was made for a music teacher, the other for a skate dancer.

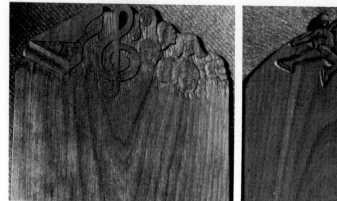

½ size – on a conch tray

Fragmentary

Actual size – on an onyx ball

Fig. 113. These Mayan motifs are from Yucatan and are similar to scrimshaw: they were engraved, then candle-smoked and polished.

shallow hollowing beneath them, the deepset eyes by sharp brow lines above, the strong jaw and thick lips by the hollowing around them. It is less effective than the Indian by T. E. Haag (Fig. 115), which uses deepened relief. The

Figs. 114 and 115. Head of Napoleon (left) is in cherry; the background was bosted and darkened. The American Indian was carved by Ted Haag.

head of Juarez in mahogany (Fig. 110), also carved there, but from a Covarrubias sketch, is about 4×6 in (10×15 cm) and almost the equivalent of a pen-and-ink sketch. Sharp edges define the nose and eyes, the collar and hairdo. Tilted V-grooves raise the lapels above the jacket and project the lips forward from the lower cheek, as well as the hair in front of the forehead. The trench groove around the head is also tilted to give a wider outside edge and visually sets the portrait ahead of the background.

The psychological study of Napoleon (Fig. 114) was somewhat tricky to design but relatively simple to carve. The background was lowered to leave a heavy self-frame on top and sides and darkened to increase apparent depth. The tricorn hat somewhat disappears in the likeness of the imperial eagle; perhaps a little less antiquing of the eagle would have been better. The face itself is entirely made up of female nudes, each modelled somewhat, but not sufficiently to overcome the accent of his features. If nothing else, this is a good way to study anatomy and practice carving the nude.

The next example is a breadboard in cherry, carved for a music teacher (Fig. 111). The central clef masks a hanging hole, and the silhouette of the grand piano on the left is matched by a series of children's heads on the right.

To separate the figures from the background, and to control the visible grain to a degree, the background is lowered and textured with roughly parallel shallow gouge cuts. Another breadboard (Fig. 112), also of cherry, shows two skate dancers, slightly more modelled. Both examples approach outlining rather than relief carving at all.

Simplest of the lining techniques is an adaptation of the old art of lithography. This was usually done on stone, shell, or ivory, the resulting grooves being flooded with ink, the surface wiped dry, and the ink in the grooves transferred to paper by pressing the latter on the design. Scrimshaw, which is usually done on whale or shark teeth, or walrus ivory, is a variant of this technique, except that scrimshaw was often done with a pointed tool like a knife or awl, so the groove was simply scratched in, while in lithography the groove is cut with a burin, the solid chisel that jewelers use in engraving. In scrimshaw, the grooves are filled with India ink or a color and then the surface is cleaned with very fine sandpaper or steel wool. A similar technique can be used on wood, providing the wood is hard and dense and the grooves are actually cut, rather than torn, into the surface. (This is the old woodcut technique, actually, except that, like a scrimshawed piece, the design is produced for itself, not as a method of transferring the design to paper or cloth.)

The lithographed onyx and shell from Mérida, in the Yucatán (Fig. 113), are variations of scrimshaw. The lines, in these cases, are made with a burin, as in lithography, but they are filled by smoking with a candle, then wiping the surface clean. The onyx ball, probably a finial for an oil lamp or the like, is an antique, and the conch shell is quite modern, but they are both made in the same way.

The essential in any work like this is a steady and sure hand, as well as a clear and clean design, because every line will show in the finished piece. When used on wood, it becomes more difficult because of the wood grain. Also, because wood is likely to be dark, the filler color should be a white oil paint, which is applied in the lines as far as possible, then allowed to dry and sanded off. The problem with wood is that it has surface pores, so the pigment may fill them as well as the carved lines, and may tend to weaken the design.

CHAPTER XVI

How to Carve Nudes

THE TYPICAL whittled human figure turned out in the United States today is a male, often fairly mature and fully clothed, usually in ill-fitting garments at that. He has three wrinkles at each elbow and knee, a sagging seat, and a smirk. A major part of the reason for this is that most whittlers haven't taken the time to learn the proportions of the human figure, and it is difficult, anyhow, to work as the sculptor in clay does: making the figure in proper proportion, developing the musculature, then applying clothing or draperies. Such a procedure is difficult when one is working from the outside in. Nevertheless, any whittler or woodcarver who is familiar with proportion will turn out a better figure, as a sculptor must.

There are certain basic proportions for the figure, some of them dating back to Greece and Rome, including: an arm span equal to the height, the foot the same length as the head, and the face the same length as the hand. We also have developed a basic guide of measuring the body in "heads": the average male is 7½ heads tall, 2 heads wide just below the shoulders, 1½ heads wide at the hips, with arms 3 heads long below the armpit, and fingertips to elbow equalling 2 heads. The average female is somewhat shorter, with narrower shoulders and a broader, shallower pelvis, hence wider hips. The narrower shoulders combine with shorter and straighter collarbones to make the neck longer and more graceful, but puts more slope in the shoulders. Also, the female neck tends to have a greater forward angle, so there is a greater tendency to look round-shouldered, particularly in older women. The female has a shorter upper arm, hence a higher elbow location and shorter overall arm length.

The male body averages 2¾ heads for the neck and trunk (½ head for the neck, or less), and 3¾ heads for the legs and feet. The feet are a head long and half a head wide. From the ground to the crotch is roughly half the height, as is the distance from the pit of the throat to the tip of the outstretched middle finger. Upper and lower legs are equal in length. The distances from the sole to the top of the kneecap, from the kneecap to the point of the *iliac* (farthest forward part of the thigh bone), and from the pit of the throat to the lower line of the *rectus abdominus* (front abdominal muscle) are equal. Roughly speaking, the body can be divided into three parts: neck to hips, hips to knee, and knee to sole. The distance from the sole to just below the knee is a quarter of the height, and the distance from top of head to pit of throat multiplied by 5½ is the total height. In the male figure, the elbow is at the top of the hipbone and the fingertips are halfway between crotch and knee. The female torso is proportionally as long as the male, but the breastbone is shorter, so the abdomen is deeper and the legs are likely to be shorter. However, in females the leg length varies so greatly that it is difficult to estimate the standing height of a woman who is sitting or kneeling.

Proportions of the figure vary widely with age, of course. At birth the center of the figure is above the navel; at two years the navel is the center; but at three the center of the figure is the top of the hipbone. It moves down steadily as the child matures, until it is level with the pubic bone in an adult male and slightly above it in the female (because of her shorter leg length). The child of one to two years is about 4 heads high, at three years is 5 heads high and at six years, 5½ heads. The child of three is about half the adult height, of ten, about three-quarters adult height. The gain in height is about one head between ages 1 and 4, 4 and 9, and 9 and 14—and remember that the head is growing larger as well. The small child's head is almost round; it lengthens in proportion as the skull enlarges. Lack of knowledge of these relationships is the reason so many primitives carve a good Madonna but a very mature Child.

While only the stoop is commonly recognized, both male and female figures change with age and posture. The female figure tends to become broader and thicker through the abdomen and hips as a result of childbearing. Both sexes tend to develop a "pot," as well as the stoop, with advancing age. Women become noticeably round-shouldered as a result of added flesh between the shoulders. Compression of cartilage between the spine segments and between joints reduces overall height, and loss of muscle tone causes general sagging. The early-adult balance of the forward projection of the chest with the rearward projection of the buttocks is lost, allowing the chest to be less prominent and the buttocks more so.

In terms of planes, the male torso is a rough trapezoid from the line of the shoulders to the nipples, almost at right angles to the sides of the body. The abdominal plane extends downward from the nipples as a rough triangle sloping inward to the navel, where it meets a plane rising from the crotch to

Figs. 116 and 117. Companion mahogany busts from the Philippines show tribal hairdos and are each about 8½ in (21 cm) tall.

the navel. In back, the line of the shoulders forms the base of a triangle that extends downward and inward to the waist, where it meets a wider trapezoidal plane rising from the buttocks. The front planes tend to have a convex curve, the back ones a slightly concave one, which is divided centrally by the groove denoting the backbone.

The female figure is basically similar in structure, except that the plane of the shoulder extends farther outward to the nipples and meets the planes of the side in a gentler curve. The frontal planes are divided by the groove of the breastbone. Note that the breasts are set at an outward angle to the front of the torso because of the curvature of the breastbone and rib cage. In the female, also, the upper-back plane slopes outward more to the lower line of the shoulders, then inward to the waist, giving greater curvature to the backbone and a greater stoop to the shoulders. While the male neck is short and thick and rises firmly from the square shoulders, the female neck is longer, more slender and more graceful, and rises at a greater forward angle. Thus, in both sexes, the line of neck to head is not vertical, but slopes forward. Also, the neck is not simply a cylinder. It tapers like a tree growing from the shoulders, more so in the male than in the female because of his normally greater shoulder-muscle development and heavier neck muscles. In addition, the male has the Adam's apple at the top. The female figure also commonly has a considerably greater outward slope to the planes of the lower back, caused by the thicker thighs and more rounded abdomen, which creates a larger diameter at the buttocks and proportionally wider hips.

Greek and Roman artists glorified the male nude, but European artists since that time have preferred the female and considered it the ultimate in artistic achievement. Instincts aside, I find the female torso largely a series of harmonious curves, while the muscular male torso is much more difficult to carve. A slight change in pose alters muscle location and size, and smoothing the muscle curves tends to make a male torso look effeminate. The female torso is affected by change of position also, but the surface effects are not nearly so evident.

These comments, of course, are intended to apply to formal and properly proportioned, as well as somewhat idealized, youthful figures; older people are rarely depicted in the nude anyway.

Artists tell me that it is not possible to sculpt the human figure without a live model and some training in anatomy, but this is not necessarily true. It is possible to create creditable nudes without formal training, although working with models is a distinct help in locating muscle positions and the like. (One difficulty is that many models are nowhere near ideal in their proportions.)

The female nude panel (Fig. 119) was carved in Tualatin, Oregon, and I present it because it is *not* the product of a school-trained carver or professional artist, and because it shows greater variety in pose and technique than I have seen elsewhere. Ted Haag has worked in the round and in relief, large and small, both formal and stylized, and he has demonstrated imagination in mounting and finishing as well. He does not believe in sandpaper, preferring to finish surfaces entirely with the tools, but his nudes are an exception. He points out that viewers tend to stroke his figures and like a silky feel. This reinforces my earlier comments about the female nude: it should be largely an assemblage of smoothly faired curves.

Ted Haag's nudes are better than mine, and better than most I've seen or judged. He provides no information on models, but the proportions look good to my eye. I am reminded that Petty, who had quite a vogue some years back in drawing the "Petty Girl," eventually admitted that he used

Figs. 118 and 119. The modern Balinese nude at left is surprisingly stumpy. Note the oversized head. The shallow-relief nude at right is by Ted Haag and is about 3 ft (90 cm) tall.

several models, one girl for upper torso, one for arms and legs, one for heads and hands—and a male model for the buttocks! The man, he felt, provided a tauter posterior.

For contrast with Mr. Haag's females, I have provided two Balinese in-the-round nudes (Figs. 118 and 120) and a Filipino couple (Figs. 116 and 117). The tendency in Bali is to attenuate figures, as can be seen elsewhere in this book, so it is a bit surprising to see a stumpy and somewhat fleshy version in the standing nude. These are both in a wood that at least is colored like mahogany.

Nudes made as panels are quite difficult because the third dimension must be flattened, and there is the ever-present possibility that the figure will look flat as a consequence. Meticulous care must be taken to produce continuous curves on surfaces. Also, the method of mounting is very important, unless the figure is a silhouette. Mr. Haag has done some experimenting in this regard with various degrees of relief for the same figure, and has also developed a shadowbox frame which is quite effective.

Fig. 120. Another modern Balinese nude, again with a head that is out of proportion with the body. It is, however, more graceful than the nude in Fig. 118.

CHAPTER XVII

An Action Sport Figure

MANY SCULPTURES are undistinguished and stiff, and so formal as to be almost unnatural. Even higher percentages of whittled pieces are similarly stiff and are misproportioned as well, so they are more caricature than statuette. Often the whittler has had no training in human proportion, had no suitable model available, was limited by a particular block shape, or was timid about cutting elements free. These may be excuses of the sculptor as well; the old Greeks often carved action figures with arms, feet or legs supported by unnatural columns, bushes, or just lumps of material.

There are subjects which can readily be spoiled if any of the preceding things are done—or mis-done. Sports figures are an excellent case in point, because the best poses involve an instantaneous freeze of a moment of supreme stress. The game of squash offers a good example because the play-

Figs. 121 and 122. Rough blanking (left) was done with a straight saw and chisels. Because the figure was small and easy to hold, whittling was the simplest method of fabrication.

119

ers are constantly in motion, and at about twice the speed of tennis. The player is frequently only slightly in contact with the playing surface, and his arms and legs are spread. Also, the racket represents a difficult sculptural element.

Thus, it was with some misgivings that I undertook a commission of and for a squash player, to be executed in mahogany. I had available an action snapshot that was taken from dead front, which of itself is rather difficult to find. (Squash courts have side walls, so most photos are taken from above, foreshortening the figure.) Because the player was obviously in contact with the floor only on the ball of one foot, with his body tilted well to the side in a turn, it seemed inadvisable to make figure and base integral. By making the base separate, I could gain both strength and contrast with the figure itself. Also, the racket projects so far across grain that it would be too fragile to withstand ordinary dusting. Thus, this figure is held to its base with a steel pin running up through the ankle at an angle designed to provide maximum support, and the racket was separately made and inserted.

A major problem was to provide a matching side view, because the legs are spread much wider than the frontal view suggests, and the elbow positions are not obvious either, nor is the twist in the back which makes the right shoulder appear narrower than the left in the front view. (This will not

Figs. 123 and 124. Rough blocking locates shoulders, hips, and limb position. Face, shoulders, feet, and hands are detailed, the right hand being shaped after the hole for the racket is drilled (right).

Fine-saw & glue in wire screening, then grind outer edge

Saw

Racquet-maple (Insert in hand)

⅜" hardwood template

Mount on steel dowel, from nail

To mount, drill template, then drill foot & base thru it

SQUASH-RACQUET PLAYER   Mahogany-walnut base

Fig. 125. Sketch and photo of finished "Squash Player." The figure is 6 in (15 cm) high over the base and was designed from a frontal photo.

be a problem for those who elect to duplicate this figure; I mention it for those who elect to depict some other sportsman in some other pose.)

Because there was no base, the entire silhouette could be sawed out to avoid a great deal of roughing. By the same token, the figure was difficult to hold in any conventional way while cutting was done, and I found it necessary to whittle much of it. Also, I made the figure somewhat heavier in build than the drawing, because the client, a squash player, is sturdy, in contrast to the thin and willowy Pakistanis who are the champions in this sport. It was obviously necessary to work carefully on the feet and arms because of the grain, and to be constantly aware of having wood available for the shirt and collar.

The racket is difficult, no matter how it is made. I elected to make it of some other wood than mahogany, to increase the strength. I used maple, stained to approximate the color of the mahogany. The stringing could have been done in several ways. The all-wood method is to thin the area within the rim, then to groove it with a veiner so that the string pattern is inverted. (Only a Balinese would attempt actual carving of the strings.) Another method would be to form the racket and drill its rim for stringing with mono-filament nylon or fine copper wire. However, I hit upon the idea of sawing the hollowed rim lengthwise with a fine-bladed jeweler's saw, then inserting a piece of aluminum fly-screen and gluing the assembly. After the glue set, the edge of the screen was ground away to leave an edge that looks very much like that of a strung racket.

CHAPTER XVIII

The Self-Made Man

A WOODCARVING OF A CARVER is quite rare. I recall only two among the thousands of designs I've seen. This is surprising, because the carver can be his own model and the material is a natural. Thus, I decided to make *Self-Made Man* from a section of 6-in (15.2-cm) walnut log and to follow the methods used by such eminent painters as Maxfield Parrish, Norman Rockwell and Andy Warhol: I took photographs from three sides to provide patterns. Further, I decided to add a fillip: I'd have me carving myself, with some of the log remaining to show the source.

The first step is to take the photographs. When the pose is selected, the photographer should focus on a level with the *center* of the subject and squarely to one side; this reduces distortion. Pictures from the front and other side should be taken at the *same* focus. Then the negatives or transparencies can be projected on paper at the desired size, and the pattern traced. (It is also possible to make photographic enlargements to the desired size, but there is usually a little distortion that makes tracing and adjustment of the various views necessary anyway.) Because of perspective and possible shifts in pose, such as a slight lowering or raising of the mallet, the patterns should be aligned, compared and adjusted before being traced on the wood.

If you are starting with a squared-up block, the views may be transferred with carbon paper; but if you start, as I did, with a log, it is necessary first to produce squared surfaces at the top and on three sides, at least (for the area of the carving only), so that the pattern can be traced. It is also advisable to square up the base at this point, so it can be used as a starting point for vertical measurement; the top will promptly be cut up. Squaring up will also reveal checks and flaws that may interfere with the carving. Small cracks can be reinforced immediately with thinned glue (like Elmer's, half and half with water), so they won't cause breaks during roughing out. Also, as you rough, any cracks revealed should be glued and/or filled before they cause trouble.

Figs. 126-129. *Two of the three photos (above), taken 90° apart, that were the basis for the pattern. The photo without shirt was to show forearm musculature. The finished pattern is also the source of front and side working patterns and templates (below), cut from light but sturdy cardboard or plastic.*

Figs. 130-133. First cuts are made at the top with hand saw and heavy chisels to clear the head and right arm; then the open area under the arm is roughed out. Removal of the waste wood between the arms is the next step, followed by a rough-shaping of the figure. The finished work is shown below right.

As usual, carving should begin at the top, with the base used for holding the piece. (On this particular log, the spongy growth-wood made clamping in a woodworking vise quite simple and flexible.) Waste wood can be cut away around the head and mallet of the figure with a cross-cut saw and flat chisel, then the back and far side are shaped. This work can be expedited by copying the drawing on heavy paper or cardboard and cutting out templates for front and side; I actually made my original sketch on heavy stock and used it (Figs. 128 and 129). Next, cut out the upper portion of the front, between the arm and head, and shape the head and the mallet for reference points for the rest of the carving. The body and arms can then be shaped. In carving the arms, be certain you retain proper lengths and proportions for the forearm and upper arm; obviously the carving will be more lifelike if the two arms match in actual length and the fists are the same size. Legs can also be rough-shaped at this point, and final decisions made about how much of the carver's body is to project from the log.

At this point, I got my nerve up to try the difficult portions of the carving —the right hand and the head, really the face—because if these two are not well done, the rest of the carving won't matter. The left hand is less important, but should be done next. This hand grips the chisel, which must be straight when viewed from its side, so it is essential to position the chisel on the leg and in the hand before the hand is finally shaped, otherwise you may have insufficient finger thickness on one side or the other. Also, it is difficult to produce a believable chip at the chisel end, particularly if the chisel is cutting at a slant into the grain, as it is in this pose. Further, the head must be tilted so that the eyes are watching, or appear to be watching, the cutting edge of the chisel—so chisel shape and position are quite important. (I found it necessary to vary a bit from my sketch at this point; you may, as well.)

Remember that, as you carve, you must leave wood for such things as the collar on the shirt, the eyeglasses and the hair, unless you plan to add them later. Shape the shirt and legs, using the photographs to locate the wrinkles in their proper places. Finish the face, carving the glasses in place and the hair (such as it is). The glasses, if you wear them, can be made separately from wire and installed; this makes carving of the face easier, but does add an element that is foreign and may cause dusting troubles later. If your figure is to have the cigar, the mouth and left cheek must be slightly distorted for it. It should be made separately and inserted in a drilled hole; otherwise it is across grain and will cause both carving and maintenance difficulties.

I chose to experiment with a different method of depicting hair, because mine is cut quite short and the usual veiner lines would suggest greater length. I put a thin layer of Elmer's glue in the major hair areas and sifted walnut sawdust on top of it until no more would stick. Then I added glue and more dust where needed. It worked out quite realistically, taking a slightly darker tone when finished.

A friend who, like several observers, missed the fact that the carver is carving himself, suggested the extension of the right leg. This was a happy thought, because it not only suggests that the figure is emerging from the log but also breaks the rigid line of the log edge. This edge can show chisel marks all around if you prefer; I showed them in front only, where he is obviously working, leaving the back of the figure quite rough in shape. (After all, how would he reach his back with the tools?)

Finish was several coats of spray matte varnish (satin) followed by two coats of wax. I had originally intended to remove the growth wood as a final operation, but decided to leave it, complete with nicks and wormholes, to strengthen the impression of a figure emerging from a log. As you probably know, the lighter growth-wood darkens when varnish is applied, so it is not disconcertingly light in the piece.

Index

accordionist, 39, 43
American Indian, 110, 111
ash, 7
assemblies, 88-92
"A Train," 47-52
Balinese carving, 73-78, 80, 117, 118
basswood, 6, 15
bee tree, 15
bench plate, 10, 11
Benito Juarez, 56, 109, 111
bird watcher, 39, 43
bosting, 12
bullfighter, 102, 104
bullnose chisel, 8, 9
canthus major, 30, 31
caricature, 22, 23, 38-46
carver's screw, 10
chimney sweep, 41, 42
chisel, 8-13, 18
Cervantes, Miguel de, 96, 97
Chamula Indians, 89, 90, 92
clasp knife, 6
composites, 88-92
Covarrubias, Miguel, 111
Danish wood oil, 52
deer dancer (of Mexico), 84, 85
DeFregger, Franz, 94
Don Quixote, 23, 42, 43, 44, 45, 46, 65, 67, 96, 97
Easter Island, 61
ebony, 17
Egyptian carvers, 23
Ellington, Duke, 51
eyes, carving the, 30-32
face, carving the, 22-37
feather dancer (of Mexico), 84, 86
"Final Chapter," 96, 97
firmer, 8, 9, 11, 12
fluter, 8, 38
fluteroni, 8
four-way head, carving the, 27
framing, 98, 99
gaucho, 66, 67
Gibbons, Grinling, 93
gouge, 8, 9, 10, 11
Gurend, Robert, 103, 107
Haag, T. E., 110, 111, 116, 117, 118

Haitian carving, 56, 77-78
hammer, 10
Hawkins, Ruth, 103, 107
head, carving the, 22-37
high-relief carving, 93-100
Hoffer, Andreas, 94
honing, 13
in-the-round carving, 5, 25, 100
Iriana (New Guinea), 84
ivory, 7
jaeger (huntsman) head, 39, 45
jelutong, 15, 46
Kjellstrom, E., 39, 41, 43
knife, for whittling, 6, 7, 12
La Malinche, 54, 57
London system of tool identification, 10-11
macaroni, 8
Macassar ebony, 78
"Madonna and Child," 65, 67, 94, 95
mahogany, 7, 16
mallet, 8, 10, 12
"Mars," 82
"Maurice," 82
Maya Indians, 27, 55, 92, 103, 106, 110
mendicant figures (of South America), 63, 64
Mérida, Yucatan, 110, 112
Mexican carving, 26, 54, 56, 102, 105, 110, 112
Michelangelo, 23
modelling, 101-112
"Moneylender, The," 97, 98, 99
naive art, 69-72
Napoleon, 111
native figures, 53-60
nose, carving the, 34-35
nude, carving the, 113-118
Oberammergau, 19, 39
panel carving, 6
Pátzcuaro (Mexico), 102, 105
penknife, 7
"Petty Girl, The," 116
pine, 6, 15, 19
point-to-point enlargement, 19, 20

portraits, 36-37
primitive carving, 5, 53, 69
profile, carving the, 33, 34-35
proportions, anatomical, 113-114
rasp, 8
riffler file, 8
Sancho Panza, 23, 26, 42, 45, 96
Sayer, Charles M., 10
Scandinavian carving, 38, 41, 42
sconce, 102, 106
scrimshaw, 110, 112
sharpening equipment, 12, 13
shellac, 8
Siva, 73
skew chisel, 8, 9, 11
sloyd, 7
South American carving, 61-68
Speckbacher, Josef, 94, 95
squares method of enlargement, 20, 21
"Squash Player," 119-122
step-by-step head, carving the, 28-30
street orchestra, 39, 40
Sutter, H. M., 10
Tarahumara Indian, 109
teak, 7, 16, 17
texturing, 37, 81-87
Tilem, Ida Bagus, 75
tool kit, 10
tools, how to choose, 6-14
"Tryst," 98, 100
Tyrol, 38, 40
veiner, 8, 9, 10, 11, 12, 38
V (or parting) tool, 8, 9, 10, 11, 12, 103
walnut, 7
"Western" carving, 47
whittling, 5, 7, 12, 18
wood, how to choose, 15-17
Yugoslav carving, 4, 69-72
Zapotec Indian, 54
Zinconteco Indian, 54